BRITAIN IN OLD PH

Perth

GAVIN & RUTH SMITH

SUTTON PUBLISHING LIMITED

Sutton Publishing Limited
Phoenix Mill · Thrupp · Stroud
Gloucestershire · GL5 2BU

First published 2000

Title page photograph: Bells' bottling and
packaging plant, *c.* 1900. (United Distillers
& Vintners)

British Library Cataloguing in Publication Data
A catalogue record for this book is available from the
British Library.

ISBN 0-7509-2381-4

Typeset in 10.5/13.5pt Photina.
Typesetting and origination by
Sutton Publishing Limited.
Printed and bound in England by
J.H. Haynes & Co. Ltd, Sparkford.

**PERTH &
KINROSS**
C O U N C I L

The authors and publishers are grateful to Perth & Kinross Council for their
assistance.

Queen's Bridge with the Tay running high, *c.* 1980. (Tom Berthon)

CONTENTS

One of the 'Provost's Lamps' outside Municipal Buildings, 1930s. The arms of Perth were first recorded in 1673, and use the red and silver colours of St John the Baptist. The Holy Lamb, associated with St John, carries the banner of St Andrew. The Latin motto *Pro Rege, Lege, et Grege* translates as 'For King, Law and People', and was a favourite of William, Prince of Orange. It is thought that Perth may have adopted this motto out of admiration for William's fight for freedom from Spanish occupation.

INTRODUCTION

'Perth, so eminent for the beauty of its situation, is a place of great antiquity, and old tradition assigns to the town the importance of a Roman foundation. That victorious nation, it is said, pretended to recognize the Tiber in the much more magnificent and navigable Tay, and to acknowledge the large level space, well known by the name of the North Inch, as having a near resemblance to their Campus Martius' – Sir Walter Scott in *The Fair Maid of Perth*.

Because of its location at the highest navigable and lowest fordable point of the River Tay, Perth played an important role in the political, ecclesiastical and commercial life of Scotland from early times. This 'Fair City' has been home to royal courts and to parliaments, and has witnessed the murder of a monarch and a narrow escape by another. If Perth was sometimes a dangerous place for kings to be, it was also close to the ancient Scone coronation site for Scottish monarchs. Of the many occasions when Perth was at the centre of Scottish life two episodes stand out, the first being the murder of King James I in 1437, and the second the sermon preached by John Knox in St John's Kirk in 1559, an event that sparked the Reformation.

For many years Blackfriars friary was pressed into service as a royal palace when members of the monarchy visited Perth. In February 1437 the court was based in the city for Christmas celebrations. On 21 February Robert Stewart of Atholl and Robert Graham, representing members of the nobility who had grown tired of James' autocratic style, led a force of 300 men against the monastery.

When Graham's cohorts broke into the royal apartments of Blackfriars, James attempted to escape via a privy, or so legend has it. Sadly for the king, however, his potential exit had been blocked up to prevent the loss of tennis balls during matches on a court outside the building, and he was captured and killed. His body was subsequently buried in the Charterhouse, where it was joined eight years later by that of his wife, Joan. Margaret Stewart, sister of Henry VIII of England and wife of James IV, was also buried there.

In his St John's Kirk sermon of 11 May 1559, John Knox exhorted the congregation to 'Purge the churches from idolatory'. Inflamed by his oratory, the worshippers proceeded to smash the altars in St John's, then set out to wreck Loretto Chapel, St Ann's Chapel and the monasteries of Greyfriars, Whitefriars, Blackfriars and Charterhouse. Only St John's remained essentially intact at the end of the day. The gateway to the Charterhouse, one of the few ecclesiastical structures to survive the events, was rebuilt as one of St John's doorways, where it remained for some 200 years.

There is an old joke to the effect that Perth is the smallest city in Scotland because it lies between two inches. The name 'inch' derives from the Gaelic for small island, and as these are low-lying areas it seems reasonable to assume that at one time the Tay did indeed cut them off. The North and South Inches are said to have been given to the town by Robert II in 1377, though there is a tradition that the powerful Mercer family gave them to the town in exchange for right of burial in St John's Kirk. An ancient rhyme says 'Folk say the Mercers tried the town to cheat/When for two inches they did win six feet'. Perhaps this is true, since the Mercers do have a family vault in the kirk.

It was on the North Inch in 1396 that Perth's infamous Battle of the Clans was fought, between representatives of the clans Kay and Chattan. The two clans had a long-standing feud and decided to settle it by armed combat between thirty men of each side. The fight took place before the king, and forty-eight of the sixty men are supposed to have been killed. The bagpipes played by the Clan Chattan piper – who was among the dead – are said to survive. Part of them – the Black Chanter – is in the Clan Macpherson Museum in Newtonmore. A fictional account of the conflict forms the climax of Scott's novel *The Fair Maid of Perth*.

Inevitably, the occasional, dramatic, wide-reaching episodes that have earned headlines for Perth through the centuries have been underpinned by the quiet, gradual and unspectacular events that shape any town or city. There has been an increase in population, expansion of the physical perimeters of the city and a widening of its commercial and industrial base.

Because of its historical importance, Perth has long been one of the major centres of population in Scotland. Its comparative prosperity has led to repeated physical development, meaning that far fewer very old buildings survive than one might imagine. Thankfully, important archaeological excavations during the 1970s succeeded in yielding a great deal of fascinating information about the origins of settlement within the city (see Chapter 1).

Trades such as weaving and dyeing were at the core of Perth's prosperity from early times, and these and other industries expanded with the coming of the railway and with improved road networks. During the nineteenth century Perth became a world centre for dry-cleaning, and also came to be at the heart of the burgeoning business of insurance.

Perth has also long been a focal point for agriculture, and its location between the scattered distilleries of the Highlands and the principal whisky markets of the Lowlands and England led to the city playing a major part in the whisky industry. The involvement of local families led to the likes of Bell's and Dewar's becoming household names around the world (see Chapter 4).

Some 90 per cent of the population of Scotland live within 90 minutes travelling time of Perth, and the city's desirable location attracted a number of large companies to locate there during the closing years of the twentieth century. Sadly, however, the ebb and flow of increasingly global commerce also saw the city's importance in the whisky industry greatly diminished.

And finally, is the 'Fair City' really a city at all? Officialdom may insist that it is not, but the people of Perth cite the 'Golden Charter' granted by King James VI in 1600 as evidence for their case. In this document he describes Perth as 'a free city and a regal and royal burgh'. That is good enough for most citizens, and anyway, the 'Fair Town' doesn't have quite the same ring to it . . .

1

Early History

Archaeological excavations on the site of
Wallace's department store, 1982.

Althougth the first surviving written record of the burgh of Perth dates from the early twelfth century, by that time Perth was already a prosperous and thriving settlement. The oldest existing burgh charter is from 1209, by which time woollen manufacture and milling were well established.

The origins of Perth were much earlier than written testimony might suggest. The name is thought to be derived from the Celtic for a wood or copse, and part of a Pictish cross was dug up in a garden in Brompton Terrace, while an earth-house came to light at Barnhill in the early 1900s. Remains of a prehistoric dwelling and a midden were discovered on a High Street site during the 1950s, and a prehistoric canoe dating from between 8,000 and 6,000 BC was found near the present harbour.

It is known that by the start of King David I's reign in 1124 there was a flourishing community based on Watergate and High Street. Skinnergate, Kirkgate and South Street were also in existence during the twelfth century. The burgh boundary in medieval times consisted of the Tay and the Lade, which surrounded it on three sides, and entry to the town was through several gates, or ports. The Lade is an ancient canal that runs from the River Almond to the River Tay, and it effectively gave Perth a defensive moat. A castle stood on the approximate site of the present Museum & Art Gallery, but it was swept away in a flood of 1209, when King William I was lucky to escape with his life (see Chapter 2).

In 1298 the English king Edward I took the city, after defeating the forces of William Wallace. He proceeded to fortify the settlement, building an impressive defensive wall. The city was held by the English forces until 1313, when its freedom was gained by Robert the Bruce's army, and the wall was subsequently demolished. Bruce spent a considerable amount of time in Perth until his death in 1329, renting accommodation for his physician and even his pet lion, according to the Exchequer Rolls. In 1336 large-scale re-fortification took place under Edward III of England, which lasted until the eighteenth century.

Prior to the Reformation Perth boasted four friaries, and so was an important ecclesiastical centre. The Dominican friary of Blackfriars (situated around the junction of the present Carpenter and Kinnoull streets) was founded in 1231 by King Alexander II. It was used as a meeting place for the General Council of the church, and it was in Blackfriars that James I was murdered in 1437 (see Introduction). Eight years before James' death the Charterhouse had been founded by his wife, Joan of Beaufort, and thirty years later Greyfriars was established by the Oliphant family. Part of their land became Perth's burial ground in 1580. The city's fourth friary was Whitefriars, which was established in 1268 by the Bishop of Dunkeld.

Perth was as important a location in political circles as it was in ecclesiastical ones, and Blackfriars played host to a number of Scottish parliaments. The significance of Perth in medieval Scotland is illustrated by the fact that a major treaty was signed there in 1266, in which Magnus IV of Norway ceded the Hebrides and the Isle of Man to Scotland. Many monarchs were well acquainted with Perth, and for a time it was effectively Scotland's capital and parliamentary centre. The last four 'Perth parliaments' met during the first half of the seventeenth century.

The present St John's Kirk dates from the fifteenth century, and is Perth's only surviving medieval building, though there was a church on the site from at least 1126. Two major events led to the destruction of most of Perth's medieval buildings, firstly the widespread damage caused in the wake of John Knox's sermon of 1559 (see Introduction), and secondly the occupation of the city by the forces of Oliver Cromwell in 1651.

In August 1651 Oliver Cromwell negotiated the surrender of Perth while in Scotland in pursuit of Charles II, who had been crowned at Scone earlier in the year. The following year Cromwell built a citadel on the South Inch, approximately where Marshall Place and Edinburgh Road have their junction today. Many buildings were demolished to provide stone for the citadel, including 140 houses and the original King James VI Hospital at the east end of the High Street. Garden walls, gravestones, the town cross and remains of the 1617 bridge over the Tay were all consumed by the vast construction project. After the Restoration of the monarchy in 1660, the structure was partially demolished, though it was briefly re-fortified by the Jacobites in 1715 and again in 1745. During the rising of 1715 the 'Old Pretender' spent three weeks in Perth in January 1716, hoping he might be crowned James VIII at Scone, before being forced to retreat to exile in France.

In September 1745 Charles Edward Stuart paraded his troops on the North Inch, before heading for England and his abortive attempt to restore the Stuarts to the throne. Prince Charles stayed in the house of Viscount Stormont – the High Street site is now occupied by the Royal Bank of Scotland – for eight days. It seems that the Jacobites were not the most popular of visitors, as Charlie raised £500 for the fighting fund from sometimes unenthusiastic local sources, and took the Provost prisoner – only letting him go when the Jacobite army reached Auchterarder!

During the 1560s the population of the burgh had been between 5,500 and 6,000, but a rise in numbers towards the end of the eighteenth century caused Perth to develop beyond the confines of its medieval limits into what we now think of as 'Georgian Perth'. By the time of the first official census in 1801 the city's population had risen to 15,000. Thirty years later the figure stood at 20,000.

Expansion took place principally to the north and south of the old settlement, with Rose Terrace, Atholl Crescent and Atholl Place all facing the North Inch, while King's Place and King James' Place overlooked the South Inch. Charlotte Street and Charlotte Place were also Georgian developments, while George Street was opened in 1773 to provide an approach from the High Street to the new Perth Bridge built by Smeaton over the Tay (see Chapter 2). Of all British cities, only Edinburgh and Bath can boast a better stock of surviving Georgian architecture than Perth.

Remains of the Parliament House, High Street, January 1976. During the mid-1970s archaeological exploration took place on the site now occupied by the Marks & Spencer store. The work was sponsored by the Scottish Development Department, and produced a great deal of fascinating information about urban life in medieval Scotland. Artefacts discovered date from the twelfth to fourteenth centuries, though the Parliament House itself was built in the late sixteenth century, and probably hosted four parliaments between 1606 and 1651.

Day-old chick meets 450-year-old egg! The egg dates from the Middle Ages, and was discovered during excavations on the High Street site which took place during 1975–6. Remarkably, the egg was recovered intact. Subsequent excavations included the High Street/King Edward Street site now occupied by Fraser's store, the Whitefriars and Blackfriars sites and areas of Mill Street, North Methven Street, Tay Street/Canal Street, Kirk Close, Meal Vennel and the site on Canal Street where the multi-storey car park now stands.

A skeleton discovered during the excavation of the Whitefriars site, 1970s. The Carmelite House of the Whitefriars once contained the residence of the Bishop of Dunkeld, who founded it in 1268, but unfortunately no trace of this was found during the dig. What were discovered, however, were the remains of eleven burials. Ten of the bodies had been conventionally buried, but the skeleton of the eleventh was found to be face down – causing speculation that he had been a murder victim.

The sole surviving section of Perth's city wall, Albert Close, between Skinnergate and George Street, 1990s. Perth was the only walled city in thirteenth-century Scotland, and the wall followed the course of present-day Canal Street, Canal Crescent, South Methven Street and Mill Street. The gates in the town wall were removed in 1764, the same year in which the Mercat Cross, which stood on the High Street at the junction with Kirkgate and Skinnergate, was removed. The wall was finally demolished in 1766.

Scone Palace, 1920s. Scone Palace is the home of the Earls of Mansfield, and was built between 1803 and 1808 on the site of an older palace. That structure had, in turn, occupied the site of the Augustine Scone Abbey, which dated from 1116–20. This was the traditional coronation site for Scottish monarchs from AD 846, when Kenneth McAlpine brought the 'Stone of Destiny' to Scone. Despite the fact that Edward I took the Stone to Westminster Abbey in 1296, Scottish kings continued to be crowned at Scone until 1424, and Charles II was crowned there in 1651, nine years before his English coronation.

The earliest known seal of the Burgh of Perth, early fifteenth century. Examples survive appended to the charters of several religious houses. After converting to Christianity, the Picts consecrated Perth church and bridge to John the Baptist, hence the alternative name of St Johnstoun. The obverse of the seal (left) depicts the beheading of St John, while Salome stands by with a platter, ready to receive his head. This seal was used until the Reformation.

Huntingtower Castle, 1970s. Huntingtower dates principally from the fifteenth century, and in 1487 the Ruthven family of Huntingtower was raised to the peerage. In 1581 the 4th Lord Ruthven became the first Earl of Gowrie. The following year – during the Ruthven Raid – the earl and his supporters held the young King James VI in the castle to try to persuade him not to support a rival political faction. Once released, James had Gowrie executed, and took his ultimate revenge on the family as a result of the 'Gowrie Conspiracy' of August 1600. This event took place in Gowrie House, dating from 1520, situated on the site in Tay Street now occupied by County Buildings.

Gowrie House, 1791. King James was lured to Gowrie House by the Master of Ruthven, younger brother to the 3rd Earl of Gowrie, either by an announcement of the discovery of a large amount of gold or, more controversially, by promises of homosexual favours. Once at Gowrie House the king was reputedly the victim of an assassination attempt. Whether this was true, or merely an opportunity to discredit the house of Gowrie, remains one of the great mysteries of Scottish history. The earl and his brother were both killed, the family estates were forfeited and the Ruthven name proscribed.

Fair Maid's House, Curfew Row, *c.* 1912. Sir Walter Scott portrayed Catharine Glover – The Fair Maid – as living there in 1396, when there was a property on the site. In 1629 the influential Glovers' Incorporation of Perth acquired the house and used it as a meeting place for more than a century and a half. The Glovers was one of nine 'incorporated trades' that were active in Perth, and their motto 'Grace and Peace' is carved in Gothic style above the door. The building was renovated in 1893–4, and very little of the original medieval structure has survived.

Fair Maid's sculpture, High Street, 1990s. There is nothing to suggest that the figure of Perth's most famous daughter is anything other than a figment of Sir Walter Scott's imagination. This does not, however, prevent the occasional drunk from taking a seat beside the sculpted figure and attempting to strike up a conversation.

Prospectus Civitatis Perthi, from John Sleezer's *Theatrum Scotiae*, 1693. Perth viewed from the east bank of the Tay, with St John's Kirk prominent in the middle of the engraving. Note the absence of a bridge, and that the gardens of houses in Watergate run down to the river, long before the construction of Tay Street on their land.

Water Vennel, between Watergate and Tay Street, 1990s. Before the creation of Tay Street the Water Vennel was a right of way to the River Tay between the wealthy houses of the Watergate, which was *the* place to live in medieval Perth. Tay Street was created between 1870 and 1875, and in the mid-1960s the Earl of Kinnoull's early seventeenth-century town house in Watergate was demolished.

Vennel names reflect the importance of medieval trades, hence Salt Vennel, Ropemakers' Close, Meal Vennel, Fleshers' Vennel and Baxters' Vennel.

Entrance to Fleshers' Vennel, 1999. The irony of the accompanying advert is presumably unintentional! Fleshers' Vennel led from South Street to the Fleshmarket, held in medieval times in the market area adjacent to St John's Kirk. It lies in the heart of the commercial area of the early settlement. The fleshers, or butchers, were a powerful force in medieval Perth, and nearby Cow Vennel may take its name from the same trade, although this was an established route to the South Inch for grazing, and the cows in question may well have been kept for dairy purposes.

St Ann's Lane, 1990s. St Ann's was one
of the 'kirk vennels' which ran from
South Street to St John's, passing partly
through a medieval kirkyard. The Chapel
of St Ann – mother of the Virgin Mary –
was once located on the site that was
later occupied by the Grammar School.
The word vennel is from the French for
lane or alley, and the only other Scots
town to use the term is Dumfries.

Cutlog Vennel, formerly called Murdieson's Vennel, was an important thoroughfare in medieval
times, leading to a northern gateway in the city wall. The name 'Cutlog' could come from the old
Scots word 'cutlug', meaning lodgings for troops. For many years there was a guardhouse on the
south side of High Street, opposite the vennel entrance. It has also been suggested that in medieval
times roads were often 'paved' with tree trunks which had been split down the centre and
embedded into the ground.

A view of Perth from the north, 1776, prior to the construction of Rose Terrace, Charlotte Street and other Georgian developments. Cattle graze on the North Inch, and clothes are being washed on the river bank. Both the North and South Inches were regularly used for washing, drying and bleaching purposes, and during the nineteenth century a watchman was employed to guard clothes drying overnight. The role of the Inch for laundry purposes diminished with the opening of a public wash-house on Mill Street. The salmon landed by the rowing boat would surely be the envy of any Tay angler today!

A view of Perth from the south, 1824. In the foreground the citizens of Perth are enjoying themselves on the slopes of Friarton Hill, but in the centre of this aquatint the buildings of Perth Prison, dating from the Napoleonic Wars, are clearly visible. Most of the vessels on the river are sailing ships, but the boat heading for Dundee on the right of the picture is clearly powered by steam. It may well be the *Tay*, which became the first steamboat to operate between Perth and Dundee in 1814.

Statue of Thomas Hay Marshall, Marshall Monument, 1990s. The Marshall Monument is incorporated into the present Museum and Art Gallery, and was erected by the citizens of Perth to commemorate their former Lord Provost. It was designed in the style of the Pantheon in Rome. Thomas Hay Marshall was a member of an eminent Perth family, and is generally credited with creating the Georgian 'new' town, though plans were drawn up and land bought by his father-in-law, Thomas Anderson.

Rose Terrace, 1970s. Rose Terrace is one of the architectural gems of Georgian Perth, and, like many of the buildings erected at the time, it was the work of Robert Reid (1776–1865). In addition to Rose Terrace, Reid was responsible for Atholl Place, Atholl Crescent, King's Place and King James' Place, the last two being modelled on London Street, which he had built in Edinburgh. The former Academy is a fine example of the architecture of the time, featuring Venetian windows and Doric pilasters.

High Street looking west, 1841. Skinnergate is on the right, and St John's Street on the left. Over the years High Street property numbers have altered, and what was no. 34 in this lithograph is now 44. The structure currently houses a building society office. This was the very heart of the medieval city, though St John's Street was added during the period of Georgian expansion and development.

George Street, looking north, 1841. Most of the buildings on George Street survive to this day, though the block to the left of the Marshall Monument was demolished in the early 1930s to make way for the new Museum and Art Gallery. It is interesting to compare this picture with the photograph of George Street in 1930 on page 115.

2

Rivers, Bridges & Floods

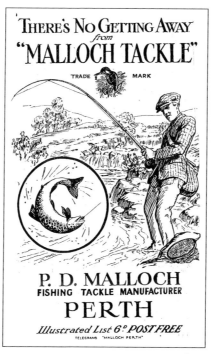

A 1925 advert for P.D. Malloch, whose Scott Street shop was a mecca to anglers for generations. The business survives, and is now in the old High Street.

At 116 miles, the Tay is Scotland's longest river. Its catchment area covers 3,000 square miles, and it discharges more water into the sea than the Thames and Severn combined. The Tay is, historically, one of the great salmon rivers of the world, and it also made Perth a somewhat unlikely commercial port. For a time, too, it was a centre for shipbuilding, with timber for boat construction being floated downriver from forests in Highland Perthshire.

Perth was the lowest bridging point of the river until the construction of the Tay bridges and, although there is no hard evidence to support its existence, the first Perth Bridge was reputedly a wooden structure, said to have been built by Agricola in AD 78.

If the river has been a positive factor in the history and development of Perth, it has unquestionably had its negative side, too. Flooding has been an element of Perth life since at least the early thirteenth century.

The earliest recorded flooding of Perth took place during the Feast of Michaelmas in 1209, an event recorded by the great Scottish historian John of Fordun in his late fourteenth-century *Scotichronicon*. 'It is said that the rivers Tay and Almond became so much swollen, that the town of Perth was almost wholly inundated. A large mound or hillock (situated at the old junction of the Almond and Tay) was forced down by the waters, and overthrew not only several houses, but the bridge over the Tay, and an old chapel.'

It was not until 1329 that a new stone bridge was built, replacing the ferry service which had previously operated. The new bridge was damaged by floods in 1573, 1582 and 1589, before finally being destroyed in 1607.

Between 1599 and 1617 a ten-arch bridge in line with the High Street was built to the design of Perth architect John Milne. The river soon found weaknesses in this structure, however, as its arches were insufficiently wide to allow the flow of flood water through. Just four years after its completion Milne's bridge was destroyed. After this, the people of Perth seem to have bowed to the apparently irresistible forces of nature, and from 1621 until 1771 river crossings were made by ferry.

The lack of a bridge was finally addressed as Perth expanded during the Georgian era, partly owing to the efforts of the Earl of Kinnoull, who personally contributed £500 to the building project. Construction began in 1766 and the bridge was completed five years later, at a cost of £26,000.

Although the Perth Bridge built by Smeaton withstood the worst the Tay could throw at it, flooding continued to be a perennial problem, and the highest level of flooding was recorded in February 1814, when ice built up against the piers of Perth Bridge, almost damming the river. Water reached as far as New Row and ice remained on the North Inch until the following summer.

The worst flood in modern times, however, occurred in January 1993, when the second highest level in history was recorded. It was brought about when a sudden temperature rise after heavy snowfalls led to a rapid thaw. Snowstorms began on Monday the 11th, and by Sunday the 17th the city was badly flooded. In the Horse Cross, next to the Museum and Art Gallery, cars were almost submerged, and the

North Inch was soon totally under water. The South Inch had already been flooded, partly by the Craigie Burn. The 1993 flood is estimated to have cost the community £40 million, and led to the development of the Perth Flood Prevention Scheme.

The stranger to Perth is often amazed to find that a city more than 20 miles from the sea has a working harbour, but rivers were of great importance for import and export purposes in days when roads were little more than tracks.

A Royal Charter of 1137 first promoted the harbour, allowing the import of flax and the export of leather goods and hides. Perth lies at the head of navigation on the Tay, facing Western Europe, and by the end of the thirteenth century it had links with the Netherlands and towns in the Hanseatic League. Perth traded on a regular basis with Italy, Spain, France, Germany, the Netherlands, Russia and Scandinavia during the eighteenth century, when flaxseed, linseed and flax were imported for the area's expanding textile industry.

The original harbour was situated at the east end of High Street, in an area known as the 'North Shore', but owing to progressive silting and the development of larger ships, it has moved further south as time has passed. Sometime after 1600 it was transferred to a site adjacent to Greyfriars burial ground, where the Lade ran into the river, originally called South Shore, and later Coal Shore. In 1752 the quayage was extended southwards to a point opposite the South Inch. This was the Merchant Quay. The present harbour site has been used since about 1840, with the tidal basin being completed five years later.

By the early nineteenth century trade was declining, because the sand and gravel banks were an obstacle to increasingly bigger vessels, although work was undertaken after the creation of the tidal basin to improve navigation. The development of the rail network from the mid-nineteenth century also helped to accelerate the river's commercial decline, though the harbour was extended in 1898 and again in 1939.

Many cargoes were sent from Dundee to Perth by rail, with ships docking in Dundee. By this time steam-powered vessels were becoming popular, and their draught was too great for the comparatively shallow waters of the Tay at Perth.

In the mid-1950s a degree of maritime prosperity returned to Perth Harbour, as by this time the design of vessels that might trade to Perth had altered again, being diesel-powered and built with shallow draught. Today the continuing viability of Perth Harbour owes much to its proximity to the modern motorway network.

An etching of Perth Bridge, with a tower in the garden of Gowrie House on the left of the picture, 1775. At this time Perth Bridge would still have been a recent innovation, and a number of vessels appear to be anchored between Gowrie House and the bridge, at the old harbour area known as the North Shore.

An engraving of the River Tay at Perth, 1830s. The Waterworks (background, left) was a recent addition to the city skyline, having opened in 1832. In his 1793 book *Journey Through Parts of Scotland*, Robert Heron noted, on approaching Perth by coach from Aberdeen, 'Immediately under the town appear the masts of vessels, numbers of which are commonly either lying in this station, or moving up and down the river.'

An aerial view of the Tay at Perth, looking north, showing Perth and Queen's bridges, 1977.

The folly on Kinnoull Hill, with the River Tay, west of Perth, to the right, undated. Kinnoull Tower, a folly, was built as a 'ruined tower' in 1829 by Lord Grey of Kinfauns, in imitation of similar follies that he had seen along the River Rhine in Germany.

Kinfauns Castle and the River Tay, with Perth in the background, undated. Kinfauns Castle was built between 1820 and 1822 for Francis, 14th Lord Gray. It passed by inheritance into the family of the Earls of Moray, and was later sold. It is now a hotel.

Perth Bridge from Bridgend, with Victoria Bridge and part of the Railway Bridge (1864) in the background. Perth Bridge was designed by the well-respected engineer John Smeaton, who constructed a very similar one over the Tweed at Berwick, and was also the architect of the Forth & Clyde Canal. The run-down hamlet of Bridgend began to thrive in the wake of the bridge's completion. The writer and traveller Thomas Pennant called Smeaton's creation 'the most beautiful structure of its kind in North Britain', though he criticized it for being too narrow. This was partially remedied in 1869, when footpaths were added.

The gravestone of John Mylne at Greyfriars burial ground. Mylne was Master Mason to King James VI, and was responsible for rebuilding the bridge swept away by floodwater in 1621.

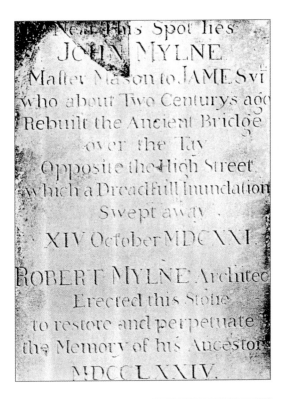

The plaque on the parapet of Perth Bridge, dating from its widening in 1869. John Pullar was Lord Provost at the time. The nine-arch structure is built of red sandstone, and the circular 'in-fills' that are apparent in the stonework today were originally channels designed to allow water to flow through in the event of an extremely powerful flood, and so relieve pressure on the bridge.

The North Inch during flooding, 31 January 1903. The Lynedoch Memorial (to the Perthshire Volunteers) is in the background.

An artistic shot of the South Inch during flooding, 1880. In the extreme left of the photograph the wooden studio of celebrated Perth photographer Magnus Jackson can just be seen. In 1886 this studio was demolished to make way for St Leonards-in-the-Fields church, and Jackson moved to new, grander premises in 60 Princes Street, which still exist.

Victoria Bridge, 1920s. In 1900 Victoria Bridge opened in line with South Street, but sixty years later it was replaced by the Queen's Bridge, constructed from pre-stressed concrete.

Police attend an accident involving an overturned lorry on Queen's Bridge, 1962.

The Tay in spate, with Kinnoull parish church and primary school in the background, 28 January 1974.

Perth Bridge, 1974. Two residents examine plaques marking high water levels. The highest mark commemorates the flood of 1814, when the river – still blocked by ice – was unable to cope with a sudden, rapid thaw.

Flooding in North Muirton, 1993. More than 1,200 houses were damaged in North Muirton, and two road bridges and the railway bridge were closed for a short time. There was serious concern for the safety of the Queen's Bridge, in particular. Houses remained unoccupied for weeks because of the need to clean and dry them out, and also because of extreme demands on local tradesmen. In some cases it was seven months before people returned to their homes.

The North Inch, May 1999. After 800 years of recorded flooding, the £22 million Perth Flood Prevention Scheme was devised in 1995, and work began in late 1998 to create flood embankments and ensure that the scenes witnessed in 1993 would not be repeated.

The River Tay and Perth Bridge, mid-1960s. Note Commercial Street in Bridgend before redevelopment.

Tay Street from Perth Bridge, May 1999. The avenue of lime trees that features in the photograph above has been felled in readiness for work on the Flood Prevention Scheme.

Launching ceremony for the *Jessie Meck*, Perth Shipyard, 1872. Shipbuilding was recorded in Perth from 1774, but it was during the first half of the following century that the industry thrived, with 400 boats being built between 1800 and 1879, when the last sizeable sailing ship – the *Ballinbreich Castle* – was launched. During 1837 five quite large vessels were simultaneously under construction, and at about this date Graham's shipyard, which employed sixty carpenters, and Brown's Cow Inch yard, dating from 1821, were very active. By the time a 36-ton steamship, christened *Bertha*, was launched in 1896, Perth's shipbuilding industry was all but at an end.

Perth Harbour, *c*. 1870. In the foreground a number of fishermen appear to be trying their luck, while a formally attired artist captures the scene. To the left of the harbour is Perth Prison, which was originally built in 1811 to guard French soldiers captured during the Napoleonic Wars. In 1842 it re-opened as the first General Service Prison in Scotland, housing 328 prisoners.

A busy scene at Perth Harbour, April 1985. Today animal feedstuff is the principal imported cargo, along with coal, coke and chemicals, steel, timber, limestone, wheat, fertilizers and road salt. Imports have risen from just under 79,000 tonnes sixteen years ago to in excess of 214,000, but exports have fallen from more than 28,000 tonnes to just over 4,000 during the same period. Even as recently as the mid-1990s, Perth was exporting coal, coke, cement and animal feed, but today the principal export is barytes. During 1999/2000 more than 236,000 tonnes of cargo was handled, and 185 vessels visited the harbour.

Loading potatoes at the harbour, late 1890s. For many years Perth had a thriving trade exporting potatoes by sea to London. Potatoes had originally been grown in large quantities to sell to the French prisoners of war held in Perth Prison. When they returned home after the Napoleonic Wars a new 'export' market for the surplus crops was developed. During the early 1900s cargoes discharged at Perth included timber from North America, Russia, Germany, Finland, Sweden and Norway, cement from Edinburgh, paving stones from Thurso, slates from Wales, roofing tiles from Belgium, tram rails from Newcastle and tramway setts from Sweden.

The *Cleopatra* pleasure steamer on the Tay, 1890s. The *Cleopatra* was one of a number of steamers that worked between Perth and Dundee, calling at Newburgh and other riverside piers en route. Unlike most of her fellow craft the *Cleopatra* survived requisitioning during the First World War, and continued to sail the Tay until the 1930s.

The heaviest recorded salmon caught by a rod in British waters remains Georgina Ballantine's 64 lb, 4 ft 6 in long fish, caught near her home in the old ferryman's house by the new Caputh Bridge on 7 October 1922. In 1973, 14,076 salmon were caught by rod in the Tay river system, but by 1998 that figure had fallen to 8,474. As well as salmon fishing by rod and line, there was also a thriving local seasonal salmon fishery when the fish were plentiful. It involved several hundred men, working from fishing stations on both banks, using small boats and nets.

A pearl fisher working on the Tay, undated. The glass-bottomed bucket helps the fisherman to see mussels, and the wooden pole is to lift them from the river bed. During the period 1761–4 the value of pearls from the Tay that were shipped to London totalled some £10,000. One of the finest Tay pearls was found by Bill Abernethy in 1967. An average pearl weighs about 10 grains, but the Abernethy Pearl weighed 33 grains. It is now owned by Cairncross of Perth, the long-established St John's Street jewellers.

3

Road & Rail

The former head office of Stagecoach plc on
Charlotte Street before the company moved
to new office premises on Dunkeld Road in
the 1990s.

By the late eighteenth century the road network in much of Scotland had been developed to quite a dramatic extent, and in 1837 an anonymous Perth contributor to the *New Statistical Account of Scotland* (published in 1845) was able to write that 'The turnpike roads in the parish, from south to north, are about four miles and a half, and from east to west about two miles. The roads diverge from the city as a centre, – one to Edinburgh, on the south; two to Glasgow, on the west; and one to Dunkeld, Inverness, &c. on the north; one to Aberdeen on the north-east. They are not now as they were formerly, ill made and ill kept. They are made and kept in repair entirely upon Mr McAdam's judicious system, to the incalculable benefit and comfort of the traveller. On all these roads, four-horse coaches run daily.'

The same writer also noted that 'A rail-road between Perth and Dundee is projected; surveys have been taken, and some subscriptions raised to carry the project into effect. But it does not meet with the concurrence of several of the proprietors, through whose parks and pleasure-grounds it would require to be carried; and some obstacles will stand in the way of bringing it to the city, which it will not be easy to surmount. It is not, therefore, probable that the work will be at present proceeded in; and the more especially, as the improvements in the river navigation promise to make water conveyance both more rapid and more frequent.'

The work was, however, 'proceeded in', and the Dundee & Perth Railway came to town in 1847, with the original station being at Barnhill, to the east of the River Tay. The first railway bridge was a swing bridge, which could open to allow boats to progress up river, and once this was completed a station was constructed on Princes Street, operating well into the twentieth century.

In 1848 the Scottish Central Railway (later to become absorbed into the Caledonian Railway) connected Perth with Glasgow, and the company constructed the present General station. The possibility of building it on the South Inch was explored, but problems of gradient and opposition from local people prevented this. The station was enlarged in 1866 and completely redeveloped twenty years later, when the Station Hotel was added.

Also in 1848 Perth was linked to the capital by the Edinburgh and Northern Railway. This line operated via a ferry across the Firth of Forth at Burntisland, until the opening of the Forth Rail Bridge, when the North British Railway ran a service from Edinburgh via Glenfarg. Lines soon opened to Aberdeen (Scottish Midland Railway) and Inverness (Inverness & Perth Junction Railway), and a network of local lines was also developed. The Highland Line was built between 1861 and 1863 linking Birnam with Forres, and ultimately Inverness. The more direct, surviving route from Perth to Inverness over Slochd Summit dates from the end of the nineteenth century.

The development of the railway network allowed Perth to capitalize fully on its location for the first time, and large quantities of freight passed through the city, in addition to large numbers of passengers. 'Whisky trains' were a common sight, and during 1867 up to 21,000 sheep per week were passing through Perth during the sales season en route to markets in the Lowlands and England.

Prior to 1923 three major Scottish railways served Perth – namely the Caledonian, North British and Highland. A series of amalgamations in 1923 reduced these to just two operating companies – LMS and LNER. At one time each of the three railways had its own locomotive sheds, one of which was one of the largest in Scotland, and each ran its own separate goods yards, making the railways a major employer in the city.

As a reminder of the heyday of railway operations, Tay Street Bridge continues to be painted in the green and cream livery of LNER, the last private railway to operate through Perth and Dundee. Prior to 1923 this operation was controlled by the Caledonian Railway Co. King's Place Bridge remains painted in the maroon and black livery of LMS.

Perth's role as a gateway to the Highlands for thousands of summer tourists, in addition to its year-round role as a busy commercial and retail centre, led to serious road congestion in the city before the introduction of one-way systems, parking restrictions and other traffic-flow improvements, and ultimately the construction of Friarton Bridge and the Western Bypass.

It is worth bearing in mind, however, that traffic congestion in Perth is not purely a twentieth-century problem. The market cross that stood at the point where the High Street crossed the medieval thoroughfare along Kirkgate and Skinnergate was removed in 1765 because it obstructed the passage of coaches. The cross was sold at auction for just over £5, and reputedly resides in a Perthshire garden.

Britain's motorway developments of the second half of the twentieth century mirror the railway network expansion that had taken place a century earlier, and Perth's attractiveness as a domestic and business location owes much to the network of modern roads that surround it.

During the late nineteenth century the city's suburban expansion was encouraged by the development of a tramway system, which replaced horse buses with horse-drawn trams in 1895. Electric trams came into service in 1905 and ran until 1929, when they were superseded by motor buses.

Perth continues to have a major involvement in transport through Stagecoach plc, a company founded by Perth brother and sister Ann Gloag and Brian Souter with two buses in 1980. Stagecoach now employs some 45,000 people around the world.

An aerial view of southern Perth, featuring the railway station in the centre of the picture, 1970s. To the left of the north-bound railway line in the top of the picture is Dewar's East Bond, prior to demolition. The Dewar's site originally boasted its own rail sidings, and large quantities of whisky were shipped south from Perth by train.

Scottish Central Railway locomotive no. 7, photographed at Perth when new in 1862. The 'Scottish Central' railway line opened in May 1848 – before Perth station was built – and ran some 45 miles from Perth to a junction with the Edinburgh & Glasgow Railway at Greenhill, between Castlecary and Falkirk.

Perth from Barnhill showing the railway bridge and the crossing of Moncreiffe Island, *c.* 1919. A Dundee train stands in the foreground. The 1,160 ft long railway bridge was constructed in 1864, and was built across the northern end of Moncrieffe island, carrying the Dundee to Perth railway line. Prior to its creation, rail passengers for Perth had to cross the Tay from Barnhill by ferry.

The railway bridge and Barnhill, 1920s. The number of allotments on Moncreiffe Island seems to have increased from the previous picture, and note the column of smoke rising from the Waterworks chimney.

Perth General station with its impressive Gothic façade before it was extended between 1884 and 1887. In *Perth – Its Annals and its Archives* (1849) David Peacock wrote 'From the number of lines converging on Perth, it has quite attained the character of a General Railway Terminus. The Scottish Central, Edinburgh and Northern, Scottish Midland, and Dundee and Perth Railways here meet together as in a common centre – the permanent terminus of Perth being undertaken by the Scottish Central Company, who contract, for instance, with the Perth Water Commissioners, for the supply of all the railways, and sublet to the others.'

Rebuilding work in progress on the railway station, *c.* 1886. An increase in passenger and freight traffic necessitated expansion to the station facilities, which included making provision for the main 'up' line, sidings and the curved Dundee platforms. Presumably the gentleman in the top hat on the bench to the right is not vainly waiting for a train!

Perth station, looking south, pre-First World War. The clock in the centre of the photograph survives, along with its partner on the southbound main line platform to the east. According to *Hunter's Guide to Perth*, written during the late 1920s, 'Each of the main platforms are fully 500 yards long. A small army of officials are kept employed throughout the year, and notwithstanding the enormous accommodation, there are times, especially when the tourist traffic is at its height in the months of July and August, when the station, vast as are its proportions, seems too small for the traffic passing backwards and forwards.'

The Highland Railway goods depot, 1880s. The former Caledonian Railway and Highland Railway freight yards are now the site of the fire station and a nearby oil distribution depot.

A sight to gladden the heart of any railway enthusiast. Highland Railway engines getting steam up at HR's locomotive sheds, off Glasgow Road, early 1900s.

The Caledonian Grampian Corridor Express ready to depart from Perth station, *c.* 1914. The locomotive was one of a series built in 1912, and was designed to need minimal replenishments of water and coal on long journeys.

The former Highland Railway goods shed, adjacent to Glasgow Road. In July 2000 it was demolished to make way for a supermarket development, despite being one of the last surviving examples of Victorian industrial premises in the city.

A busy High Street scene (looking west) from 1976. A one-way system was introduced to the High Street in 1955, and full pedestrianization between Kinnoull Street and Skinnergate was implemented in 1990.

The junction of High Street with George Street (left foreground) and Watergate (right), prior to the demolition of buildings to make way for an extension to General Accident Insurance headquarters in 1954. The traffic is considerably lighter than in the 1976 High Street on the previous page!

High Street, 1911. This part of Perth has been central to the burgh's life since medieval times, and its importance as a throughfare is demonstrated by the bustle of pedestrians in the foreground. Despite an apparent lack of vehicles, tramlines can clearly be seen, and there appears to be some congestion in the distance. Note the diversity of businesses and the individuality of premises in the days before domination by multiple retailers.

The junction of High Street and Kinnoull Street, March 1975. To the right, construction is under way on a new building on the site of the former post office, which dated from 1898, while the Marks & Spencer store is the distinctively modern structure a few doors down. Note the presence of such once well-known retail names as Timothy White's.

South Street, looking east, with two-way traffic, 1930s. The view to the Tay was only opened up when Gowrie House was demolished in 1805. Before that South Street had ended at the junction of Speygate and Watergate. The street's importance to traffic grew dramatically with the opening of Victoria Bridge in 1900.

Friarton Bridge under construction, July 1977. The bridge opened the following year, having cost £8 million to build. Work on the project to allow traffic to and from the A85 Dundee/east-coast road to bypass the city began in April 1975.

The Craigend Interchange, prior to its opening. The interchange linked the M90 to the A85 by way of the short M85 over Friarton Bridge, and its construction necessitated the demolition of a church and cutting through part of Moncreiffe Hill.

The Scone bus, outside John Kinnear's Inn, Scone, 1880s. Horse buses of the Scone & Perth Omnibus Company made six trips each day between Perth and Scone from the 1860s until they were superseded by horse-drawn trams operated by the Perth & District Tramways Company Ltd. Trams ran between Scone and Cherrybank, via George Street, High Street and Glasgow Road, as the no. 7 bus does today.

An electric tram crosses Perth Bridge on its route from Scone to Cherrybank, via the city centre, c. 1910. Electric trams were introduced in 1905, two years after Perth Corporation took over the Perth & District Tramways Company Ltd. By this time the tram network extended along Dunkeld Road, and also to Craigie Cross.

The Perth Corporation operated motor buses in the city until 1934, when the Scottish Motor Traction company's W. Alexander & Sons subsidiary began to run Perth city services on their behalf. No. 5 was a 1928 Thornycroft, seen here when new.

Corporation Transport vehicle no. 30 was a 1933 Thornycroft Darling with a 48-seat double-decker body by Midlands Coach Works.

4

Trade & Industry

Wallace's department store, King Edward Street, 1980.

The availability of water power was a crucial factor in the growth of industry in and around Perth. Corn, lint and paper mills were established throughout Perthshire, and in the 1650s mills for grinding corn were located within Perth's walls. Their wheels were driven by the town Lade, which received its water from the River Almond. The Lade provided power and soft water, and as industry developed in Perth it grew up along the banks of this watercourse.

During the early nineteenth century Perth was one of the leading textile centres in Scotland, being involved in both linen weaving and cotton manufacturing. The level land of the Lower Tay and Almond river terraces was ideal for bleachfields.

By the middle of the nineteenth century Perth's position as a centre for textile manufacture had diminished, but the associated water-based processing industries of textile dyeing and cleaning were developing significantly. The Pullars were originally a family of weavers, and Robert Pullar started up his business in Perth in 1810, trading in waxed gingham. In 1823 his son John founded a dye-works in modest premises in Burt's Close, starting with yarn and moving into the dyeing of fabric. Later the dry-cleaning services for which 'Pullars of Perth' became famous were developed.

In the 1845 *New Statistical Account of Scotland* (in which the Perth chapter was written some eight years earlier) it is stated that:

The manufactures of Perth consist principally of cotton-coloured goods, of which umbrella cloth is the staple. A great quantity of handkerchiefs, checked and striped ginghams, imitation Indian shawls, scarfs, trimmings, &c. are also woven. The number of weavers is about 1,600. . . . Most of the umbrella cloths are sent to London, Manchester, and other towns in England and Scotland. But the other goods are generally exported to North and South America, the East and West Indies. Many of the shawl pieces are for the Turkey market.

There has lately been erected a mill for spinning flax and tow yards, containing 850 spindles. . . . The number of hands employed in it are . . . in all 103. The working hours are sixty-nine in the week. . . . Tulloch, which lies about two miles to the west of the city, is memorable from its having been the first bleachfield established in Scotland. It was established about the commencement of the eighteenth century. . . . The present proprietor of Tulloch is Hector Sandeman, Esq., who, with great integrity and enterprise, carries on an extensive bleaching and print-work. The number of hands employed is 250.

The writer also noted that until the late eighteenth century 'the glove trade of Perth was prosperous. Perth-made gloves had a preference throughout the kingdom. One tradesman had seventeen men employed in cutting out work for his sewers. The quantity yearly manufactured for home consumption was between 2,000 and 3,000 pairs. But the trade is now almost entirely gone . . .'

Gone, too, is much of Perth's involvement with the whisky industry. In the late eighteenth century Perth and its environs were home to no fewer than twenty-three small stills, but it was as a major centre for whisky blending and bottling that Perth became renowned during the last few decades of the nineteenth century. With the spread of the railway network from the mid-nineteenth century, Perth was ideally located between the distilleries of the Highlands and the markets of the Lowlands, England and beyond. It is often forgotten, however, that the city boasted its own substantial distillery, which operated from 1851 until the mid-1920s. It was called the Clockserrie or Isla distillery, and its site in Bridgend where Isla Road and Strathmore Street converge at the traffic lights is today marked by a small area of public park, gifted by Mrs A.K. Bell, widow of A.K. Bell of Arthur Bell & Sons.

Perth was put on the whisky map by the endeavours of three principal companies, those of Arthur Bell & Sons, John Dewar & Sons Ltd and Matthew Gloag of 'Famous Grouse' fame. Of the three, only Gloag's, now part of Highland Distillers, retains a prominent presence in the city, having moved to purpose-built headquarters at West Kinfauns in 1996. Matthew Gloag set up in business as a wine and spirits merchant on Atholl Street in 1820, and the name of the company's later base of Bordeaux House in Kinnoull Street reflects its role as wine shippers as well as whisky blenders and bottlers.

The recorded link between whisky and Perth dates back to 1561, when an entry in the Perth Guildry Book notes the admittance of one Ellis MacKerane – 'aquavitae maker' – to a Perth craft guild. Considering that the first written reference to Scotch whisky dates from 1494, this is a very early record of Scottish distilling.

Along with textiles and whisky, Perth has been widely associated with insurance, though, as the following pages show, the trades and industries and commercial activities of the Fair City were many and varied.

The General Accident Fire and Life Assurance Corporation was founded in 1885 by a group of Perthshire men which included several farmers, a lawyer, a banker and an estate agent. The founding of the Corporation came about as a direct result of the 1880 Employers Liability Act, and premises were acquired at 44 Tay Street. The early development of the company was due in no small measure to the drive and foresight of Francis Norie-Miller, who was appointed Secretary in 1887 and Manager two years later.

The 'GA' was the first insurance company to offer cover against burglary, and was one of the earliest to insure motor vehicles. From its modest beginnings the firm grew to become one of the leading names in insurance, as well known and well respected around the world as its expanding Perth contemporaries Bell's and Dewar's. It retained its independence for longer than either distiller, however, and finally merged with Commercial Union in 1998 to form CGU, employing some 800 people in Perth. In February 2000 CGU merged with Norwich Union, and though Perth could no longer claim to be the 'World Headquarters' of the company, as it had until 1998, the newly created insurance giant has maintained a presence in Perth at Pitheavlis.

Arthur Bell, 1880s. Arthur Bell joined the Perth wine and spirits merchants operated in Kirkside – now South St John's Place – by T.H. Sandeman in 1840, and eleven years later set up in business on his own account from the same premises. Bell was one of the early pioneers in mixing malt and grain spirit to produce blended whiskies, and by the 1890s Bell's was selling in India, Australia and New Zealand, as well as having strong markets in Europe. Arthur Bell died in 1900, leaving his eldest son Arthur Kinmond – 'AK' – to head the business.

Bell's premises in Victoria Street, late 1950s. Arthur Bell & Sons moved from Kirkside to Charles Street and Victoria Street in the early 1900s, where their administrative facilities were based until relocating to the newly built Cherrybank complex during the 1970s.

Staff at Bell's bottling plant, *c.* 1904. Bell's retained its independence until its takeover by Guinness in 1985, though in 1998 the Cherrybank operation was closed down, with most of the sales, marketing and distribution jobs being lost to Harlow in Essex. During the summer of 2000, however, Bell's opened the £2 million Cherrybank Centre, adjacent to its well-known Cherrybank Gardens. The centre maintains the company's connection with Perth through a permanent exhibition tracing the history of Bell's and its long association with the city.

Tommy Dewar, *c.* 1910. Tommy Dewar was a son of John Dewar, who had set up in business on the High Street in 1846, having previously spent eighteen years working in a wine merchant's business. Tommy joined the family firm in 1885, five years after his father had died, and he was temperamentally perfectly suited to his role as a flamboyant whisky salesman. His brother, John, stayed at home and ran the company, while 'Whisky Tom' travelled the globe, visting twenty-six countries and opening thirty-two agencies during a two-year tour from 1891 to 1893. He became one of the most famous characters in the whisky industry, and was a pioneer of advertising.

The original premises of John Dewar at 111 High Street, shortly before their demolition in 1924. The company had vacated the premises some years previously. The site was redeveloped the following year by F.W. Woolworth, who remain in the same location today. Dewar's became part of the Distillers Company Ltd the following year, finally coming into the same ownership as Bell's when Guinness acquired both Bell's and DCL during the 1980s.

George Sinclair, Thomas Donald (apparently the foreman) and William Stewart, employees at Dewar's Speygate Bond, 1891. Today Dewar's maintains a presence in Perthshire through its Aberfeldy Distillery and associated 'World of Whisky' centre.

Dewar's East Bond Warehouse, decorated as part of the peace celebrations, 1919. The warehouse had been built in 1912, when Dewar's moved from the centre of the city to a large site adjacent to the railway line, between Glasgow Road and Glover Street. Dewar's Bond remained a Perth landmark until its demolition in the 1980s, though the company moved to a new blending and bottling plant at Inveralmond in 1962. In 1990 that operation was closed, with production being transferred to a United Distillers' facility at Leven in Fife. As a result, 300 jobs were lost, and the site was subsequently redeveloped.

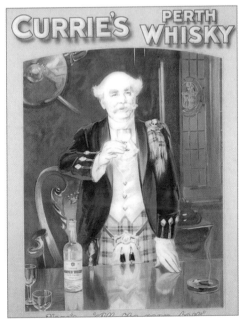

Advert for Currie's Perth Whisky, late 1920s. Currie's traded from Charles Street until 1983, when their premises were demolished to make way for the new William Low supermarket, now also gone, and three years later the firm ceased trading altogether. Until 1978 Currie's blended two whiskies themselves, and the company was actually an amalgamation of two Perth businesses – Charles C. Stuart & Son, licensed grocers, who joined in 1917 with J. & T. Currie & Co., wholesale wine and spirit merchants.

Surviving enamel signs advertising Thomson's Whisky and Thomson's Teas on an old High Street building, 1990s. The grocery and wine and spirit merchant's firm of Peter Thomson & Co. was founded by Alexander Thomson in about 1860 in premises in King Edward Street. At one time the company operated four Perth shops, but the last one closed in 1973, when they decided to concentrate on whisky blending and the wholesale wine trade. In 1973 Thomson's moved from King Edward Street to a site on Crieff Road, and the company was subsequently taken over by Waverley Vintners, now a subsidiary of Scottish & Newcastle plc, trading as Waverley.

Brewery of John Wright & Co. at 18–20 North Methven Street, 1950s. If water was important for whisky-making it was also essential for brewing, and a late Victorian advert for Wright's noted 'A unique feature of the establishment is an artesian well which for over One Hundred Years has given a supply of pure pellucid water for Brewing and Aerated Water purposes'. William Wright had established the North Methven Street brewery in 1786, and it survived until its acquisition by Vaux in 1961. Brewing returned to Perth in 1997 with the opening of the Inveralmond Brewery by Fergus and Ailish Clark.

Tayside House, Bridgend, before 1956. Tayside House was the home of Sir Robert Pullar from 1879, and later belonged to Frank Eastman, Chairman of Pullars, Edinburgh. According to the *Perthshire Advertiser* for 13 October 1937, 'Tayside, with entrance from Isla Road, and overlooking the Tay, is one of the largest and most imposing residences in the city. The house was reconstructed and considerably added to by the late Sir Robert Pullar.' General Accident bought Tayside House before the Second World War, and in 1941 the General Life Assurance Company was evacuated there from Aldwych in London.

Demolition under way on Tayside House, January 1963. General Life had remained at Tayside House until returning to London in 1956, and seven years later the mansion was knocked down to make way for a modern office block. When GA moved to its present base at Pitheavlis in 1983, the 'new' Tayside House was vacated, and now operates as a nursing home.

A portrait of Sir Robert Pullar (1828–1912) by Sir John Millais. Sir Robert was a prominent member of the dyeing and cleaning dynasty, and a committed Christian and paternalist, generously supporting many worthy causes in his native city. He was also a great advocate of temperance, calculating in 1905 that every adult in Perth spent £4 6s per year on drink – the equivalent of £2,000 per week for the city as a whole! He was elected to Parliament as a Liberal member at the age of eighty, and was made a Freeman of the City a year before his death.

An engraving of Pullar's North British Dye Works, Mill Street, 1850. The company soon outgrew its original Burt's Close premises and moved to Mill Street. By the 1860s Pullar's had diversified into dry-cleaning, and ultimately became the biggest and best-known specialist firm in the world. At one time Pullar's boasted the largest dry-cleaning machine in existence, and repaired as many as 16,000 pairs of curtains per week. In 1882 Pullar's developed a secondary site at Tulloch where they began to use benzine, a highly inflammable cleaning material which it was thought prudent to keep away from the centre of the city!

Pullar's silk stocking department, 1932. By this time Pullar's was the largest employer in Perth, with more than 2,000 people in its pay. Since 1918 the company had been owned by Eastman & Son Ltd of Acton Vale in London. This takeover followed a bitter and protracted labour dispute between the Pullar management and the Amalgamated Society of Dyers and Bleachers.

The legend 'P. & P. Campbell, Dyers & Cleaners' on an exposed gable in St Catherine's Road, 1999. For many years, P. & P. Campbell were Pullar's principal rivals, until being taken over in 1919. Campbell's premises were also situated close to the town Lade, so a ready source of processing water was always available.

Redevelopment of Pullar's Mill Street site, 2000. By the 1970s most of Pullar's dry-cleaning was being done in the firm's branch premises, and the vast Mill Street complex had become largely redundant. Some of the site was taken for local authority use, and in 2000 the rest was converted into the new £20 million Perth & Kinross Council headquarters – called Pullar House – and a multi-storey car park. The famous Pullar's chimney, often referred to as Pullars' Stalk and as much a Perth landmark as Dewar's Bond, was demolished in 1980.

An aerial view of Perth, mid-1970s, with the Mill Street premises of J. Pullar & Sons prominent. The sheer scale of the operation is evident from the air. To the left of Pullar's, on the opposite side of North Methven Street, stands the premises formerly occupied by Wright's Perth Brewery, and in the left foreground work is in progress on the redevelopment of Drumhar and adjacent areas.

Yarn passing through a warping machine at the Wallace Works, Dunkeld Road, 1936. At the time the Wallace Linen Works employed some 400 people, having been founded in Kinnoull Street in 1851 by John Shields & Co. Originally just twenty looms were in use, but new premises were acquired in North William Street as the business prospered and expanded, and in 1870 a move was made to Dunkeld Road. By 1900 no fewer than 700 looms were working, and the company employed nearly 1,000 people.

A machine transfers designs from paper to jacquard cards which control the threads and reproduce the pattern on the linen, Wallace Works, 1936. When an extension to the plant was opened in February 1900 the *Perthshire Advertiser* wrote that 'the works were famed the world over for such goods as fine damask cloth, napkins, towellings, and cotton covers. It will be remembered that on the occasion of the marriage of the Duke and Duchess of York a large supply of linen from the Wallace Works (the gift of the city of Perth) received the highest approbation of royalty.'

Jack Allen flattening the base of a piece of glassware at the Harbour Glassworks, 1950s. Glass-making in Perth dates back more than 125 years, one reason being easy access to the vital ingredient of sand from the banks of the Tay. In 1865 John Moncrieff opened a glassworks in South Street, and in 1881–2 production was transferred to a new works on St Catherine's Road. The company subsequently traded as Monax. In 1924 the decorative style of glassware known as Monart was developed, being produced until the early 1960s.

Staff at the Harbour Glassworks, 1949/50. Front, left to right: Augustine, Salvador and Vincent Ysart. Monart glassware was pioneered and made by members of the Ysart family. Vincent Ysart was born in Barcelona in about 1878, the son of a glass-blower, and he came to Scotland in 1915, beginning work with Moncrieff's company in 1924. In 1946 Salvador Ysart and two of his sons started their own business at the Shore, calling their glassware Vasart – after their own initials, Vincent, Augustine and Salvador, plus 'Art' from Ysart.

The derelict North British Glassworks premises of Monax shortly before demolition in 1999, three years after production ceased on the site. During the late 1970s the glassworks employed 140 people. Appropriately, considering Perth's history as a glass-making centre, Caithness Glass now operates a flourishing factory and visitor centre on the Inveralmond Estate.

Aerial view of Caledonian Road, 1980. The auction mart occupies the immediate foreground, and to its left is the railway goods depot. Behind that is St Catherine's Road and Monax glassworks. Note Longcauseway – between the mart and the goods yard – prior to realignment.

Aberdeen Angus cattle on show in front of MacDonald Fraser & Co. Ltd's Caledonian Road livestock market, 1930s. Modern redevelopments have seen the demolition of almost every building in this picture. MacDonald Fraser operated a livestock market in Mill Street from 1864, and in 1875 moved to prestigious new premises on Caledonian Road. The mart remained there until the creation of a purpose-built agricultural centre at West Huntingtower, which opened in 1990. Safeway's supermarket and part of St Catherine's Retail Park now occupy the old mart site.

Preparing sheep at MacDonald Fraser's mart, 1975. Perth was geographically well situated as a centre for livestock sales, with excellent rail links. As many as 800 cattle and 6,000 sheep could be sent out by train from the marshalling yards behind Glover Street after a sale at Hay & Co.'s Craigie mart. Perth continues to be an important location for livestock auctioneering, and United Auctions' annual Bull Sales in February and October comprise the largest collective sale of pedigree beef cattle in Europe. The Bull Sales were started in 1865 by John Fraser, and until 1949 animals were paraded on Caledonian Road.

Lady Georgina Home-Drummond lays the foundation stone for General Buildings, the new General Accident head offices, 25 July 1899. By this date the success of GA meant that it had outgrown its original premises at 44 Tay Street, and the former post office site at the foot of the High Street was acquired and the building demolished. The new head offices cost £2,000 to construct and equip.

The accounts department of General Buildings, early 1900s. By the early 1980s the GA had become too large even for General Buildings, despite the addition of a major extension in 1954. A new world headquarters was constructed on a greenfield site at Pitheavlis at a cost of £33 million, and the company moved out of the city centre in 1983, leaving the then Perth & Kinross District Council to take over General Buildings.

Francis Norie-Miller (left), 1920s. Sir Francis Norie-Miller, as he later became, was born in Stoke Newington, London, in 1859, and guided the fortunes of the GA for some sixty years, dying at Cleeve, his Perth home, in 1947. He was succeeded by his son, Stanley, who acted as Chairman and Managing Director and lived at Murrayshall, formerly a derelict mansion which his father had purchased and renovated in 1928. Stanley Norie-Miller is commemorated in the Norie-Miller Riverside Walk, situated on the east bank of the River Tay, between Perth and Queen's bridges.

Tommy Dickson (right) and Scottish motor racing legend Jim Clark at Charterhall racing circuit, 1957. Perth garage proprietor Tommy Dickson was a successful amateur racing driver for the Ecurie Ecosse team. He founded his motor business in Kirriemuir in the late 1940s, moving into Perth in 1951. In 1967 the company took over the former Coates carpet works on Dunkeld Road, creating Scotland's largest car showroom in the process. Dickson's is Scotland's longest-established Mercedes dealership, having been granted the franchise in 1958. In 1998 the company opened a new £1.5 million complex close to Inveralmond roundabout.

An advert for Frew & Company Ltd, late 1920s.
The firm of Frew was another long-established
motor dealership in the city, having been formed
in 1905. Five years after its establishment Frew's
was appointed the first Ford dealer in Scotland.
The firm's original premises were in Mill Street,
and they also operated out of Canal Street and
Glasgow Road, though for sixty years they were
based at Riggs Road. In 2000 Frew's was
acquired by Inverness-based Macrae & Dick, and
the company name was abandoned. At the time
this advert appeared in the early 1930s Frew's
premises were on Princes Street.

An advert for Valentine's Motors Ltd, late
1920s. Valentine's was one of Perth's first
car dealers, and had an agency for
Austin. They built Valentine Buildings
just before the First World War and, as
this advert shows, also owned a fleet of
charabancs. Note the address, City Hall
Square, more usually given as King
Edward Street. Valentine Buildings was
demolished as part of the St John's
Shopping Centre redevelopment.

The alleyway beside Garvie & Syme's High Street shop, 1975. The firm of Garvie & Syme was established by John Roy in 1856 in premises at 42 (now 52) High Street. In 1962, however, the business was consolidated in the site at 85 High Street, where it remained until transferring to Glenearn Road in 1975.

The premises of A. & G. Cairncross at 6 St John's Street, 1890s. The jewellery company was established in 1869, and in 1911 moved to its present location at 18 St John's Street.

Wallace's Department Store, shortly before demolition in 1980. By the time of its closure the store, on the corner of High Street and King Edward Street, was owned by the House of Fraser group. It was replaced by the present House of Fraser premises. The early 1960s development to the left of Wallace's was demolished when the St John's Centre was created. Note the survival of the former fire station 'tower': the left-hand section of Wallace's building was the city's fire station until 1971. The Woolworth's store on the High Street was redeveloped in 1966, having originally opened on the same site in 1925.

The interior of MacArthur's licensed grocery shop at 28 North Methven Street, between 1895 and 1902. The bottles on the counter to the left are labelled 'MacArthur & Sons Highland Whisky, Perth'. At the time it was common for even small-scale retailers to bottle their own-label whisky, or have it bottled for them. Imagine the distress of modern-day health inspectors at the uncovered meat on the counter!

Davidson's chemist shop on George Street, *c.* 1980. The company was founded by Walter Davidson in Blairgowrie in 1897, and now boasts nineteen pharmacies and five animal health outlets, though the George Street shop has closed.

WINDSOR Restaurant and Tea Rooms

Visitors to the Windsor will appreciate the excellent cooking, the comfort and daintiness of the rooms, etc., and the attentions of an efficient staff.

Music, 12.30 to 2 and 4 to 5.30

FULLY LICENSED.

James Hewat & Son, Ltd.
'PHONE 269.

An advert for James Hewat's Windsor Restaurant and Tea Rooms, early 1930s. 'The Windsor' was situated at 36 and 40 St John's Street, in premises now occupied by Brennan's pub.

The Salutation Hotel, South Street, 1990s. The Salutation Hotel was founded in 1699, having been built by Viscount Stormont as a private house in 1600. None of the original structure remains. Prince Charles Edward Stuart reputedly stayed in the hotel while marching south with his Jacobite army in 1745. Writing of 'inns and alehouses', the Perth contributor to *The New Statistical Account* of 1845 noted that 'The number of these in the parish is 249. As to their effects on the morals of the people, I have no hesitation in saying that they are most lamentable.'

The County Place Hotel, now the New County, *c.* 1900. The hotel later extended into what was then Branch No. 1 of the City of Perth Co-operative Society Ltd. The Perth 'Co-op' was founded in 1871 in Thimblerow, with ninety members and capital of £85. During its first year of operation the organization took £704 in sales, and in 1887 it moved to new premises on Scott Street. The hotel stabling at the rear of the County is now its car park, and a programme of expansion and major upgrading during 1999–2000 saw the hotel also extend into the adjacent former Ladbroke's betting office.

THE

STATION HOTEL

Is ideal Headquarters for the Tourist wishing to spend a few days in this picturesque and romantic county. Adjoining the Station, it gives the Tourist easy access by rail as well as by road to such beauty spots as Rumbling Bridge, St Fillans, Blairgowrie, for the far-famed Beech Hedges at Meikleour; Crieff, Dunkeld, Pitlochry, Callander, Dunblane, Aberfeldy and Lochearnhead.

Hot and Cold Water all Bedrooms.

OWN GARAGE.

Accommodation for 30 Cars.

Enlarged and Modernized Dining Room.

Handsome Bathrooms.

TELEPHONE 741   En Pension Terms
(3 Lines).   on Application.

An advert for the Station Hotel, late 1920s. The Station Hotel was constructed during the 1880s, when the railway station itself was being expanded. At one time there was direct access from the hotel to the railway platforms.

5

Daily Life

A corner of old Perth, 1970s.

In common with most cities and large towns the physical appearance of Perth has altered dramatically over the years, with a trend during the last two decades of the twentieth century for many businesses and services to locate outside the city centre. The construction of the St John's Centre during the mid-1980s brought a new dimension to retailing in Perth, and there were major redevelopments of both commercial and residential property in the city from the 1970s onwards.

There were significant changes, too, in local government, with the reorganization of 1975 making Perth part of Perth & Kinross District, within the newly created Tayside Region, and in the process the old title of Lord Provost was lost.

The physical provision of services has also altered, with the Tayside Police Western Division Headquarters being established on part of the former Queen's Barracks site. This multi-storey building combined the City and County Area Offices which had previously been located in the centre of the city. A new and greatly enlarged fire station was constructed at 401 High Street, near Feus Road, and finally in 2000 many Perth & Kinross Council functions were concentrated in the new council Pullar House headquarters on the former Pullar's site on Mill Street/ Kinnoull Street.

In terms of housing, nineteenth-century suburban expansion included the lower slopes of Kinnoull Hill, Craigie and Burghmuir. This expansion was encouraged by the development of the tramway system (see Chapter 3). Again, the advent of trams to Scone stimulated housing development between Bridgend and Scone. Similarly, a ribbon development of houses along Glasgow Road spread to Cherrybank once the tram service was established.

After the First World War council houses were built in Friarton, Craigie, Darnhall, Riggs Road, Hillyland, the Dunkeld Road area, and Scott Street, while the Gannochy scheme (see page 101) was regarded as one of the best in the country. The last scheme to be completed before the Second World War was Crieff Road, which included Hunter Crescent, while construction work began on the Muirton estate, though this was only completed after the war.

Post-war schemes included Moncrieff, Woodside and Potterhill, in addition to Letham, Tulloch and finally North Muirton. During the early 1990s the Crieff Road scheme was redeveloped at a cost of £19.5 million, and renamed Fairfield. Private housing developments also took place, most notably at Oakbank, Upper Kinnoull, Craigie, Muirton and on the Western Edge.

In 1960 Perth's first multi-storey flats – in Pomarium – rose up against the skyline. They were built on the site of old houses in Pomarium Street, which took its name from the pomarium, or apple orchard, of the Carthusian monastery which was situated nearby until the Reformation.

Perth was one of the earliest Scottish burghs to enjoy the benefits of gas lighting, with the first supply commencing in 1824. Eight years later the people were also able to enjoy the luxury of a safe, guaranteed public supply of fresh water for the first time. Prior to the construction of a waterworks in 1832, they had obtained their water from the town Lade, the Tay, and from private wells.

The waterworks was situated at the junction of Tay Street and Marshall Place, and was designed by Perth Academy Rector Dr Adam Anderson. The building incorporated a distinctive Georgian rotunda, and the accompanying column, topped by classical urn, was the chimney for the steam pump. The Latin motto 'Aquam igne et aqua haurio' above the door translates as 'I draw water by fire and water', and was chalked by Anderson on the wall a few days before he died.

The water supply was pumped from a well on Moncrieffe Island to the tall storage tank, and according to the New Statistical Account 'It is raised into this reservoir by steam engine power and from thence it is conducted in pipes through the streets. It is at the option of the inhabitants to take it into their dwellings.'

The city's first waterworks became redundant in 1965 after a modern replacement was built, and an engine house which had been added to the original structure was demolished in 1973 when restoration work on the premises began. The building was used initially as a tourist information centre, and now houses the Fergusson Gallery (see Chapter 6).

The construction of the waterworks did not prevent an outbreak of cholera in 1832, however, and in total 148 people died. The cholera epidemic was widespread, and its effects, along with those of several smallpox outbreaks, led to the creation of many infirmaries throughout Scotland, and Perth was no exception.

The County & City Infirmary was built on York Place in 1836, and was the first public hospital in Perthshire. Some ten years previously, however, 'James Murray's Royal Asylum' had been created. James Murray, a labourer, inherited a large sum of money. Having no immediate family to whom he could leave his fortune, he decided it should be put to good use by building an asylum on Kinnoull Hill. It should be set up, he insisted, so that 'the meanest patient could be well fed and clothed, and those among the higher classes who could pay for it were as well lodged and cared for as they could be in a palace'. The asylum cost upwards of £40,000 to build, and opened in 1827.

Education had a high priority in Perth from a very early time, and the Grammar School was in existence by 1150. The abbot of Dunfermline Abbey was responsible for the appointment of its master. The Grammar School master at the time of the Reformation was Andrew Simpson, a highly regarded teacher, and author of a standard Latin textbook. By 1760, however, there was a feeling that the Grammar School was too traditional in the subjects it taught, and the Town Council created Perth Academy, where the curricular emphasis was on commercial and scientific subjects.

The Education Act of 1872 made schooling 'national' for the first time in Scotland, creating the Scotch Education Department, and elected School Boards were set up in each area. Elementary schools that date from the years following the Act and are still functioning include Kinnoull, Craigie, the Northern District School on Dunkeld Road – now renamed Balhousie Primary School – and the Caledonian Road School.

Perth has long been regarded as an attractive place in which to live, and the city gained an official accolade in 1990, when a report by the Glasgow Quality of Life Group gave Perth & Kinross top place in its survey of 145 non-metropolitan district councils in the country.

The site of the Old Grammar School, South Street, 1990s. The Grammar School was established by
the mid-twelfth century, and was attended by such eminent men as Charles Edward Stuart's
lieutenant-general Lord George Murray, younger brother of the Duke of Atholl. The school was
adjacent to St Ann's Lane, off South Street, which at one time was home to one of the Perth
newspapers and a coaching inn. After the school moved to Rose Terrace in 1807, the building
became Perth Theatre.

Perth Academy, Rose Terrace, 1920s. The Academy had been founded in 1760, and in 1807 it
combined with Perth Grammar School and several other educational institutions in the new Rose
Terrace buildings. The land on which Rose Terrace stands was gifted by Lord Provost Thomas Hay
Marshall, in recognition of which the street was named after his wife. His house is still at the Atholl
Street end of Rose Terrace.

Perth Academy, 1982. In 1930 work began on the construction of a new Academy at Viewlands. It opened in 1932 and was extended in 1960, its bicentenary year, by which time its total capacity had risen to 1,300. From 1950 the Academy had a 'rival' in the shape of Perth High School in North Muirton, though from 1860 until 1915 Sharp's Institution in South Methven Street had provided an alternative source of education.

Tulloch School, c. 1900. In 1882 Pullar's developed a large site at Tulloch, and constructed a 'model village' for its employees, complete with a farm and school. Note the strict segregation between boys and girls! The school building survives in expanded form as the Tulloch Institute on Tulloch Terrace.

Caledonian Road Primary School, late 1890s. This was constructed in 1892 to replace schools at North Port, and King Street and the Seymour-Munro School as the population of the area swelled, owing to the increasing importance of the railway and the establishment of the Caledonian Road auction mart. When constructed, it was the largest public school in Perth. Some of the children are barefoot, which may indicate poverty, or simply good summer weather.

The Fechney Industrial School for Boys, 1890s. The now demolished 'Fechney' opened in 1864, and had a roll of 150 boys. It taught practical skills such as carpentry, tailoring, shoemaking and gardening, and supplied bundles of firewood to the town. Perhaps the timber gathered in the foreground is awaiting conversion into kindling.

The former County & City Infirmary, York Place, 1920s. At the time this photograph was taken the building was being used as Perthshire Education Authority offices, and in 1994 it opened in its new incarnation as the A.K. Bell Library (see Chapter 6).

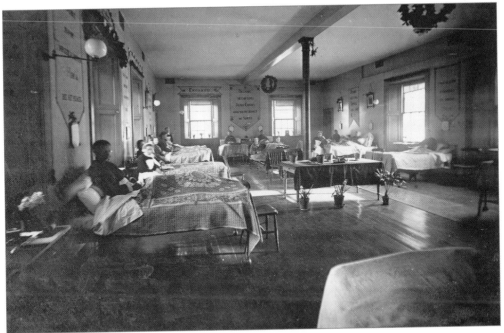

A ward of the County & City Infirmary, 1890s. The infirmary opened in 1836, having cost £6,000 to build. It was funded by public subscription, and designed for fifty-six patients, remaining the principal hospital in Perth until the opening of the Royal Infirmary in 1914. During the First World War the old infirmary was used for treating wounded soldiers, and subsequently for tuberculosis cases.

The former Accident & Emergency Department of Perth Royal Infirmary, 1973. Part of the original hospital can be seen to the left of the modern block. 'PRI' was officially opened in July 1914 by King George V and Queen Mary. According to a *Perthshire Advertiser* report of the occasion, 'When the King and Queen entered the portals of the noble building which now stands on the rising slope of Tullylumb, they found that the work of rescue and assuaging pain and suffering was in full swing and that everything was in perfect order.'

The funeral of Dewar's director Alexander John Cameron, August 1928. The funeral cortège is passing Dewar's Glasgow Road offices, where the staff have gathered, hats in hand, to pay their respects.

St John's Kirk, 1920s. The only surviving medieval building in Perth, St John's is dedicated to St John the Baptist. The first written record relating to the church dates from the 1120s, and most famously it was the place where John Knox preached his sermon in 1559 that precipitated the Reformation (see Chapter 1). Note in the foreground the junction of Princes Street and South Street, with the site of the old Grammar School and St Ann's Lane opposite.

St Leonard's-in-the-Fields Church, Marshall Place, 1920s. St Leonard's was built in 1886 on the site of the great Perth photographic pioneer Magnus Jackson's wooden photographic studio.

St Paul's Church, South Methven
Street, 1979. St Paul's has been
unused since 1986, though in 2000
there were plans to restore the
building and convert it for
community use. St Paul's is the
second-oldest church in Perth,
dating from 1807.

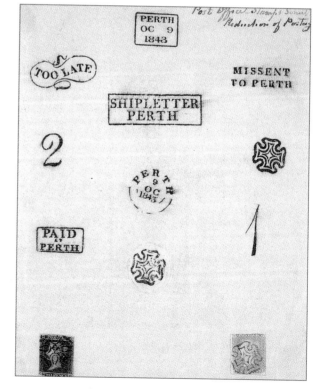

Perth Post Office stamps, *c.* 1843.
The first regular public postal
service to and from Perth was
established between the city and
Edinburgh in 1689. The
introduction of the 'Penny Post' in
1840 caused a dramatic increase in
the use of the postal service
throughout Britain. The new rate
came into effect on 10 January
1840 and, reporting on the events
of that day, the *Perthshire Courier*
noted 'nearly four times the average
number [of letters] at this time of
year' were sent, of which more than
85 per cent were pre-paid at the
new rate.

The building to the right of the Marshall Monument, Museum and Gallery (80 George Street) was once Perth post office. The structure dates from about 1784, and served as the post office until a new one was opened on the corner of High Street and Tay Street in 1862.

Perth post office, at the foot of the High Street, *c.* 1890. This site was later acquired by General Accident for their world headquarters, and the post office moved in 1898 to the junction of the High Street with Scott Street. In 1973 it made its final move to its present South Street site.

Perth Savings Bank headquarters building, Tay Street, 1880s. Perth Savings Bank was founded in 1815, and occupied its Tay Street premises in 1876. According to the *New Statistical Account* of 1845 'The investments are generally made by the labouring classes out of their savings'. At the time of the publication of the *Account* Perth boasted two provincial banks in the shape of the Perth Bank and the Central Bank, and branches of the British Linen, the Bank of Scotland, the Commercial and the National banks. In the summer of 2000 the 'B'-listed former Savings Bank building became a public house, named the Capital Asset.

A late nineteenth-century street scene in Perth, with a police officer on the left. The location is 'McFarlane's Corner', the junction of High Street and South Methven Street.

A group of three policemen, pre-1914. The centre figure is Inspector John Scott, who later became Chief Constable of Perth City Police. The city force had been founded in 1811, and survived until 1964, when it became part of Perth & Kinross Constabulary.

A late nineteenth-century Perth City Police officer, identity unknown. In 1975 Perth & Kinross Constabulary merged with Dundee & Angus to form the present Tayside Police force, which has its Western Division headquarters in Perth.

Perth Fire Brigade, *c.* 1890. This volunteer brigade fought Perth blazes until 1920, when a professional fire service was formed, initially being based at the Municipal Offices on Tay Street. A new fire station was subsequently created in King Edward Street, on the site now occupied by Waterstone's bookshop. It remained there until 1971. As far back as 1859 Pullar's had their own dedicated fire brigade, based at 16 Kinnoull Street.

An advert for Perth Corporation Gas Department, 1930s. The provision of gas in Perth dates back to 1824, when a company was formed to supply it, building a gasworks in Scott Street. A rival company later erected a gasworks in Blackfriars Street, though the two rivals amalgamated in 1868. In 1871 the Gas Commission acquired the operation, and new works in Friarton opened in 1901.

A replica of the Old Cross, King Edward Street, late 1920s. Erected in 1913 in King Edward Street as a memorial to Edward VII, this was a replica of the old Mercat Cross which stood in the middle of the High Street – between Skinnergate and Kirkgate. The original had been demolished by Cromwell and incorporated into the citadel which he built on the South Inch. A new cross was put in place following the Restoration of the monarchy.

Proclamation ceremony at the Market Cross, King Edward Street, announcing the accession of the Prince of Wales to the throne as Edward VIII, 23 January 1936. The late King George V was the first Colonel-in-Chief of the Black Watch, serving in that capacity from 1912. Pullar's chimney is in the background, and the fire station, with its distinctive 'tower', occupies the left part of Wallace's building on the right. Wallace's slogan 'The Store of Satisfaction' can just be made out on the extreme right of their premises. King Edward Street was one of the city centre's more modern streets, having only been created in the early years of the twentieth century.

HM The Queen during a visit to Perth on 12 October 1960. The Queen officially opened the new Queen's Bridge while in the city, which that day was also celebrating the precise 750th anniversary of the granting of its charter by King William I.

HRH the Duke of Edinburgh on a 'royal walkabout' in Perth during a Silver Jubilee celebration visit, May 1977. The party is passing down St John's Street, with the Kirk on the right.

Municipal Buildings, corner of High Street and Tay Street, 1920s. The buildings date from 1876, but were destroyed by fire in 1895 and subsequently rebuilt. At the time of the photograph they contained an impressive council chamber, court room, committee rooms, city chamberlain's office and the town clerk's office, along with the police station, which fronted on to Tay Street.

The County Buildings, Tay Street, including the Court House, 1920s. The County Buildings – complete with Grecian Doric portico – were erected in 1819 on the site of Gowrie House, which had extended from Water Vennel to Canal Street. Gowrie House was the scene of the famous 'Gowrie Conspiracy' of 1600 (see Chapter 1), and it was demolished in 1805 to make way for the County Buildings.

Labour Exchange, King Edward Street, early 1930s. A new Labour Exchange in Alexandra Street was opened in December 1937, replacing existing facilities in King Edward Street and the Masonic Hall at 77 High Street. The Alexandra Street premises have been converted for residential use, and bear the rare monogram of Edward VIII.

The statue of Sir Walter Scott which now stands at the Marshall Place/King's Place entrance to the South Inch in its original position at the east end of the High Street, before increasing traffic brought about its removal. The statue was purchased by the Town Council for the sum of £10, a great bargain even in 1845, and only possible because the Cochrane brothers who made the statue planned to emigrate to the USA and urgently needed money.

Perth 'worthy' Blue Cam Kate at the South Street 'port', 1880s. Kate peddled cam, the soft stone used on doorsteps, around the streets of Perth, and lived in a house in Canal Street. Sadly the rather splendid wrought-iron gentlemen's lavatory in the centre of the photograph was removed between the two world wars as it was an obstruction to traffic.

The present City Hall, soon after its opening in 1911. The City Hall was constructed at a cost of £30,000, and had a seating capacity in excess of 2,000. It replaced the previous City Hall of 1845, which was in very poor repair by the early years of the twentieth century. Perth & Kinross Council has considered the possibility of knocking down the 'new' City Hall and redeveloping the area, building a new hall and conference centre at Horse Cross – next to the site of the Museum and Art Gallery.

Derelict properties, Shuttlefield Close, *c.* 1890. As the name suggests, Shuttlefield Close was once at the heart of Perth's weaving quarter, and by the late nineteenth century its houses were in very poor condition. Much of this area was demolished to make way for the creation of 'new' Scott Street – between South Street and High Street. This photograph was the work of Magnus Jackson, and despite the fact that it has obviously been staged, it gives a sense of living conditions for some citizens of the Fair City during the nineteenth century.

Demolition work on the High Street site adjoining General Accident's General Buildings, prior to constructing a GA extension, 1954. Note the existence of firms such as Wood's, the baker and biscuit manufacturer, and Gowan's grocery and wine merchant, not to mention a branch of Pullar's. An archaeological dig on the site uncovered remains of a prehistoric dwelling and midden.

The entrance to Spey Court, with adjacent Canal Street land being cleared in preparation for the construction of Perth's first multi-storey car park. The properties in Spey Court were built on the site of Arthur Bell & Son's bonded warehouse, which was destroyed in 1919 in one of the most spectacular fires ever seen in Perth. After the fire Bell's built a new, larger bond in nearby Charles Street, and constructed a court of flats on the vacant Canal Street site. Before the Canal Street car park was built an archaeological dig discovered a kiln, probably used for malting or drying grain for brewing purposes.

Mill Wynd redevelopment, including restoration of Hal o'the Wynd's House, 1980. The Lower City Mills is on the extreme left. It has been suggested that as the house is built in a non-vernacular style it could have been constructed by Flemish weavers, who settled in this area of Perth towards the end of the seventeenth century.

Hal o'the Wynd's House after the completion of restoration work. In Sir Walter Scott's *The Fair Maid of Perth* Hal (or Henry) Smith, is an armourer who fights with Clan Chattan during the Battle of the Clans (see Introduction), and finally wins the hand of Catharine Glover, the Fair Maid of the title. Scott's novel is set in the late fourteenth century, but the present Hal o'the Wynd's House is believed to date from the late seventeenth or early eighteenth century, so any connection between the property and Hal is merely a Victorian fancy.

A derelict shop in Mill Street, adjoining the Old Granary, 1975. The shop was demolished during redevelopment, though the Old Granary has been restored. The Upper City Mills date from the mid-eighteenth century, and received a civic award when the structure was restored and converted into hotel accommodation by the Reo Stakis Organisation in 1971.

Redevelopment of Commercial Street, Bridgend, completed in 1978. Potterhill Flats, to the rear, date from 1960.

Derelict properties prior to demolition, on the corner of Back Wynd/East Bridge Street, Bridgend, February 1979.

The demolition of the same properties in progress, viewed from Gowrie Street, March 1980.

Strang's chemist's shop, founded in 1849, shortly before demolition to make way for part of the St John's Centre development. The street is Meal Vennel, which connected the High Street with South Street, one of the oldest streets in Perth. Meal Vennel disappeared as a result of the creation of the shopping centre.

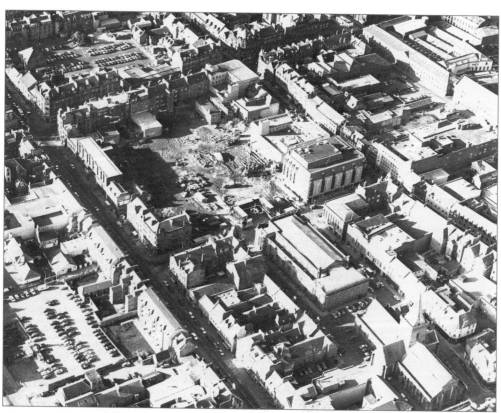

Aerial view of city centre, with the site for St John's Centre being cleared, mid-1980s. St John's Centre cost £20 million to create, and opened in 1987.

A postcard addressed to Mr William Smith, Longcauseway, Perth. The message on the reverse reads 'South West St John's Women's Guild, January 1919'; the location is unknown. Before its restoration in 1926 St John's Kirk was divided into three churches, East, Middle and West, and the reference may well be to the Women's Guild of St John's West Church.

The Gannochy Estate, 1960s. A.K. Bell purchased the Gannochy Estate during the 1920s and proceeded to build 150 'model cottages for the deserving poor'. Bell's philanthropic activities were formalised in the Gannochy Trust in 1937.

Looking north over Crieff Road and Tulloch, 1920s. Since the photograph was taken this area of Perth has been heavily developed for housing.

Perth from Craigie Hill, 1909. As with the above picture of the opposite side of the city, the most striking change between the view from Craigie Hill 'then and now' is the physical expansion that has taken place, though Craigie had already seen suburban development during the late nineteenth century.

6

Leisure

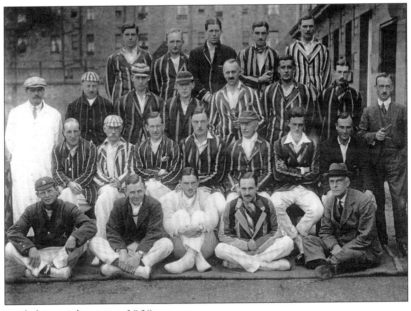

Perthshire cricket team, 1930s.

Both the North and South Inches traditionally served a number of practical domestic purposes, such as for clothes-drying and archery practice, as well as being useful areas on which to assemble armies and fight the occasional battle – as we have already seen. The Inches also, however, performed – and continue to perform – a very valuable function as recreational areas, as does Kinnoull Hill.

Even members of royalty are reputed to have enjoyed these facilities, and it is said that King James VI played golf on the North Inch. The King James VI Golf Club was founded on the Inch in 1858, moving to a new course on Moncrieffe Island in 1897.

The earliest surviving reference to Perth and golf dates from 1604, when church records note that a man by the name of Robertson was forced to sit in the seat of repentance. His crime was 'playing at the gowf on the Sabbath on the North Inch at the time of preaching'.

The North Inch was also supposedly the first place in Scotland where cricket was played, and in fact Perthshire Cricket Club is the oldest in Scotland, having been founded in 1826. A *Perthshire Advertiser* report of 1924 noted 'Perth is one of the few places in Scotland where cricket probably makes an equal appeal to football . . .'.

Horse-racing meetings were held on the North Inch during the eighteenth and nineteenth centuries, before Scone Palace Park opened in 1908. The annual race meeting of the Perth Hunt attracted the 'great and the good' of Perthshire society, and there is a record of racing taking place as far back as 1613, though no venue is specified.

For the people of Perth, the attractions of the North Inch grew further with the opening of Bell's Sports Centre in 1967, followed in 1979 by the neighbouring Gannochy Pavilion. The creation of this centre and the Pavilion was owing to the generosity of the Gannochy Trust, a charitable body founded in 1937 by Arthur Kinmont 'A.K.' Bell to do good works in Perth and the county of Perthshire. The Trust spent £225,000 building Bell's Sports Centre – a significant sum in the mid-1960s.

'A.K.' as he was almost universally known, was a son of the whisky firm's founder Arthur Bell, and he began the family and company interest in sports in Perth. He was a keen and talented cricketer, who acted as secretary to Perthshire CCC, which he also later captained. In fact, at the age of fifty-five 'A.K.' scored a century for Perth Cricket Club!

In 1925 he created a cricket ground for the people of Perth in Doo'cot Park, close to his father's old residence of Kincarrathie House. Not only was a pavilion built and cricket pitches laid out, but 'A.K.' even paid for the services of a groundsman.

Today, cricket no longer has 'equal appeal' to football in Scotland, and Perth is most widely known in sporting circles for its Premier League football team. St Johnstone FC was founded in 1884 by members of St Johnstone Cricket Club, and was admitted to the Scottish League in 1911/12. The team played at the Recreation Ground on Edinburgh Road, opposite the prison, until Muirton Park on Dunkeld Road was opened in 1924. In that year the team was promoted to the First Division of the league. Originally designed to hold 30,000 people, at one stage Muirton Park's capacity was reduced to just 2,500 in the wake of new safety regulations.

In 1989 Saints moved to a new 10,000 seater stadium at MacDiarmid Park, off Crieff Road, after Asda acquired the Muirton Park site for a supermarket development. The new ground was named after the late Bruce MacDiarmid, the Perthshire farmer who donated the land.

For many years Dunkeld Road was something of a mecca for leisure activities in Perth. In 1887 public swimming baths were established there, and in 1936 an ice rink opened next to Muirton Park, on the site now occupied by McDonald's. It soon became established as the premier curling centre in Scotland, staging the Scottish Curling Championships, and before the Second World War was also home to Perth's two professional ice hockey teams, Perth Panthers and Perth Black Hawks.

In 1990 this was replaced by Dewar's Rinks, on Glasgow Road, constructed next to the new Leisure Pool on part of the site of the former great red-brick Dewar's blending and bottling complex. This had been a distinctive Perth landmark since before the First World War. The new rink continued Perth's association with top curling competitions. The Scottish and European Championships are staged there, and in 1995 it hosted the World Junior Curling Championships.

Between 1932 and 1935 a new Museum and Art Gallery was built, adjoining the Hay Marshall building, replacing the museum in Tay Street. This 'Marshall Monument' dates from 1822, and was modelled on the Parthenon in Rome. It was erected by the people of Perth in recognition of the role played by Marshall in the expansion and development of the city.

The former waterworks on the corner of Tay Street and Marshall Place is now an extension of the museum service. The Fergusson Gallery contains a collection of work by the prominent Scottish colourist J.D. Fergusson, including some 200 oil paintings, with an estimated value of £30 million. The gallery opened in March 1992 and was voted Scottish Museum of the Year in its first year of operation.

The current Perth Theatre is also of historical interest. It dates from 1900, when it was built on the site of the Morrisonian Church, and it was refurbished in 1980–1. In 1831 the violinist Paganini played at the Theatre Royal (on the corner of Atholl Street and Kinnoull Street). One local newspaper called it 'the greatest event in the musical history of Perth'. The theatre dated from 1822, but only survived for a couple of decades. Construction of the old City Hall (opened in 1845) was probably instrumental in its demise. When its role as a theatre ended the building became clothing manufacture workshops, and subsequently home to a manufacturing stationers. It is now one of Perth's best-known restaurants.

A race meeting on the North Inch, 1890s. According to a contributor to *Chambers Journal* in October 1906, 'Once a year the great Perth Hunt meeting of all the notabilities in Perthshire, with friends from the adjacent kingdom of Fife, took place on the adjacent North Inch of Perth. Races of more or less merit were viewed from the grandstand by by ladies of high degree, while the lords and the lairds congregated about the steward's box or the then small ring. . . . In the evenings, the County Rooms at Perth are crowded with "stalwart men and bonnie lasses", dancing "high and disposedly" . . .'.

An aerial view of Bell's Sports Centre, 1977. Construction of the Gannochy Pavilion is under way to the right of the centre.

McNeil McLeay's 1842 view of the South Inch, featuring its famous avenue of elm trees, leading to the Waterworks and Marshall Place. When plans were put forward for the construction of a railway station on the South Inch during the mid-1840s, opponents used McLeay's painting as propaganda for their cause.

The bowling green, South Inch, 1920s.

Perth Cricket Club, *c.* 1930. A.K. Bell is in the back row, third from the right.

Southern District School football team, winners of the Perth School Cup, 1923/4. Southern District School was situated in South William Street and Nelson Street.

Perth Corporation public swimming baths, Dunkeld Road, 1890s. In 1886 land was rented from Lord Kinnoull to create formal swimming baths on the site of a popular bathing pool next to the Lade. The Swimming Bath Movement was founded by Sir Robert Pullar, who gave an initial grant of £250, and four years later cleared its debts of £500.

The interior of the swimming baths, soon after opening. This photograph was the work of Magnus Jackson, who was a driving force behind the creation of the baths, and a director until shortly before his death in 1891. During the 1930s new baths were built alongside the existing ones, and these were extended after the Second World War. In 1962 the pool was again extended, making it suitable for international competitions. In 1988 Perth Leisure Pool in Glover Street replaced the old swimming baths, the site of which is now occupied by the Royal Bank of Scotland.

Aerial view of Muirton, featuring Muirton Park football ground in the centre of the picture, 1980. The ice rink is to its left.

The Rodney Pavilion, and assembled General Accident staff, *c.* 1935. The Pavilion opened as General Accident's social and athletic club in 1934, and its popular, though unofficial, name was taken from Rodney Lodge, which had been demolished to make way for the new Victoria Bridge in 1900. It, in turn, was named after the late eighteenth-century naval hero, Admiral George Rodney. When General Accident moved to their new site at Pitheavlis the Pavilion was gifted to the city, and is now a fitness centre.

Buckie Braes was bought for the city in July 1914 and developed for leisure use. The Braes – a small glen close to where two streams meet to form the Craigie Burn – was a popular place for generations of Perth children to play and for family outings. Trams, and later motor buses, ran from the city to Cherrybank, and gave easy access to Buckie Braes. According to a City of Perth advert for 'Recreative Attractions' from the late 1920s, 'This popular resort, known as "the Children's Paradise," contains Refreshment Rooms, Swings, See-Saws, Maypole, Pond, and Excellent Facilities for Picnic Parties.'

The presentation of Kinnoull Hill to the city of Perth by Lord Dewar, 10 September 1924. John Dewar (later 2nd Lord Forteviot) is the central, standing figure, accepting the gift on behalf of Perth in his role as Lord Provost. Tommy Dewar is seated to his left, and John Alexander Dewar (1st Lord Forteviot) is seated on the extreme right of the picture. The people of Perth had long enjoyed free access to much of Kinnoull Hill, courtesy of Lord Kinnoull, but, as the *Perthshire Advertiser* noted, 'at the back of our minds there was aways the dread that the estate might be sold to an alien, and the privilege of entry to the most romantic part of it summarily withdrawn'.

Entrance to Kinnoull Hill, 1920s. Kinnoull Hill was a favourite haunt of the artist Sir John Everett Millais, and several of his best-known works feature the area. New houses for well-to-do Victorian families appeared on the lower slopes of Kinnoull Hill, and one of them – called Bowerswell – belonged to the solicitor George Gray. His daughter Effie married firstly John Ruskin, and then Millais. The Millais family went to live in nearby Annat Lodge, where the famous 'Autumn Leaves' – featuring the spire of St John's Kirk – was painted. Millais reckoned that the view north from Perth Bridge was 'much better than the Riviera'.

Millais' Viewpoint by Tim Shutter, 1997 – part of the Perth Sculpture Trail. The sculpture is made of red St Bees' sandstone from the Cumbrian coast, and it takes the form of a partial Victorian-style picture frame, which literally frames the view. The painting 'Autumn Leaves' is commemorated in the fallen leaves carved on to the right-hand side of the frame. Effie and the Millais children are buried in the old Kinnoull graveyard, which is visible in the 'view'.

David Wilson's 1998 bronze, granite and stone sculpture 'Outwith, Within, Leaf', in Bellwood Riverside Park, the railway bridge in the background. The Sculpture Trail extends for a mile through the Riverside Park, Rodney Gardens, and Norie-Miller Park, and features two dozen pieces of 'public art'.

An advert for the King's Cinema, South Methven Street, late 1920s. Today the building houses the King's Bingo Club. By the late '20s Perth boasted several 'picture houses', with the Alhambra in Kinnoull Street operating from 1922. The BB Cinerama was in Victoria Street, and is now the BB Bingo Club. The Corona picture house had opened its doors in 1913 and, according to the *Perthshire Advertiser* for 15 January of that year, 'the opening of the well-appointed premises in High Street is being looked forward to with keen satisfaction by the public who are practically insatiable in their demand for pictorial entertainment'.

David Annand's High Street sculpture, erected at a cost of £10,000. The two men linked by a ring was inspired by William Soutar's poem *Nae Day Sae Dark*. Soutar was born in South Inch Terrace in 1898, and when he was four years old the family moved to Taybank Cottage on the Shore. He was educated at the Southern District School and Perth Academy, where he contributed poems to the school magazine. He served in the Royal Navy from 1916 to 1919, and then attended Edinburgh University, where he graduated with an Honours degree in English Literature in 1923.

Portrait of William Soutar by James A. Finlayson. By 1929 the spondylitis – or ossification of the spine – which had first been diagnosed during Soutar's naval service was so severe that he became bed-ridden, and until his death in October 1943 he never left the bedroom of the family house in Wilson Street. This property is now used by the library service for its writer-in-residence. A committed nationalist and pacifist, Soutar wrote widely in both Scots and English. Probably his best-known work is the collection of private diary entries which were posthumously published as *Diaries of a Dying Man*.

George Street, with the domed rotunda of the Marshall Monument in the background, right, 1930. The range of buildings to the left of the monument was demolished soon after this photograph was taken, to make way for the new Museum and Art Gallery, and the junction with Bridge Lane on the left was substantially re-aligned.

The newly opened Museum and Art Gallery, George Street, 1935. The museum and gallery adjoins the Hay Marshall Building, which was home to the Perth Literary and Antiquarian Society and Perth Library. A Natural History Museum was built on Tay Street in 1881 by the Perthshire Society of Natural Science, who subsequently gifted their collection to the city in the early 1930s. Two bequests enabled the construction of the new museum and gallery, which had space to display and store the Natural History Collection along with a growing collection of other treasures. The Natural History Museum closed in 1935.

The A.K. Bell Library, 1990s. Like Bell's Sports Centre, the A.K. Bell Library was subsidised by the Gannochy Trust, and was officially opened by HRH the Prince of Wales in 1995. The library was based in an expanded version of the old Perth Infirmary building, which dated from 1836 and replaced the 1898 Sandeman Library in Kinnoull Street. Professor Archibald Sandeman of Cambridge University – a native of Perth – left a £32,000 bequest to build and equip it with books as a public library.

7

Regiments & Wars

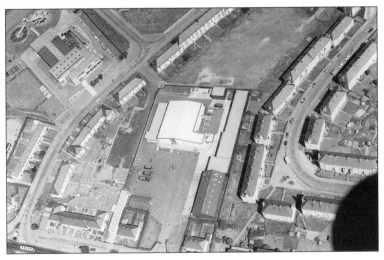

An aerial view of Dunkeld Road, featuring the new Queen's Barracks, which opened in 1975 and serve as a Territorial Army base.

Because of its strategic importance Perth has been fought over and occupied on a number of occasions, and the city has also served as an important military base. As we have seen, in Cromwell's time there was a garrison in the Citadel on the South Inch, which was partially re-fortified by Jacobite forces during both the 1715 and 1745 risings. In the wake of the failure of the 1745 Jacobite rising, the city of Perth gifted Gowrie House to the Duke of Cumberland, who proceeded to sell it to the government, after which it was converted into military barracks.

The Jacobite activities of 1745–6 led to a permanent presence of troops in Perth, beginning with an encampment of soldiers on the North Inch, commanded by the brother-in-law of the Duke of Cumberland – Prince of Hesse-Cassel. They stayed there for several years, and there was also stabling and other facilities on the site of the South Inch citadel.

In 1794 new barracks were constructed at the top of Atholl Street, and the 4th (Queen's Own Regiment of Dragoons) were the first incumbents, hence the name Queen's Barracks. A number of regiments subsequently occupied them, including, on several occasions, the Black Watch. In 1873 the barracks were converted from cavalry to infantry accommodation, subsequently becoming a permanent home for the Black Watch.

The Black Watch is one of Scotland's most distinguished regiments, and a fighting force still closely associated with the city of Perth today. The regiment recruits in Perthshire, Angus and Fife. The Black Watch is Scotland's senior Highland regiment, and was formed in 1739 from a number of independent Companies of Highlanders. The regiment's name comes from the fact that its principal role was to keep a watch in the Highlands for Jacobite activity, and that its soldiers wore a notably dark tartan.

The regiment (numbered the 42nd in 1751) served in the war against the French in North America during the 1750s, and during the American War of Independence from 1776 to 1783. Between 1798 and 1815 Black Watch troops were in action during the Napoleonic Wars, taking part in the Battle of Waterloo.

In 1854–5 the Black Watch fought in the Crimea, and two years later they were involved in suppressing the Indian Mutiny – during which the regiment won eight Victoria Crosses. In 1881 the 42nd and 73rd Regiments were amalgamated to form the Black Watch (Royal Highlanders) Regiment.

The Black Watch served in Egypt between 1882 and 1885, and in South Africa during the Boer War, but the First World War was to be the most costly action ever seen by the regiment. During that conflict the Black Watch fought in France and Mesopotamia, losing a total of 8,000 men, with a further 20,000 wounded. More Black Watch troops died during the First World War than in all the other campaigns in which they ever fought put together. Prior to the First World War the Black Watch had won twenty-eight Battle Honours, and by the time the war ended in 1918 it had gained a further sixty-eight Battle Honours, along with four Victoria Crosses.

The Second World War saw the regiment serving in France, Crete, North Africa, the Far East, Sicily and Italy, and after D-Day in France and Germany. It was again in action in Korea and Kenya during the early 1950s, and later in Cyprus. More recently the regiment has served several tours of duty in Northern Ireland, while Black Watch troops were also present at the end of British rule in Hong Kong in 1997. In the summer of 2000 the First Battalion of the Black Watch was posted to Germany as part of 1UK Armoured Division, equipped with Warrior armoured personnel carriers.

In addition to the Black Watch, Perth can also boast other less high-profile military associations. The Perthshire Volunteers, the 90th Light Infantry, was raised by Thomas Graham of Balgowan, later Lord Lynedoch, in 1794, on the North Inch, and the regiment subsequently became the second battalion of the Cameronians.

Lynedoch was born in 1748, and during the Peninsula War (1808–13) he commanded the victorious British troops under Wellington at the battle of Barossa. The victory was commemorated in Barossa Street and Barossa Place, close to the North Inch. In 1809 Lynedoch was made a general, and he died in 1843, at the age of ninety-five.

The Second World War saw Perthshire play host to a large contingent of Polish troops, who came to Britain after the fall of France in 1940, and in August 1941 Perth hosted a civic reception for the Polish Prime Minister and Commander-in-Chief General Sikorski.

The Poles stayed in Perthshire for some eighteen months, until October 1942, when they left to participate in re-forming a Polish army in Russia. According to the *Perthshire Advertiser* for 14 October 1942, a set of trumpet banners was presented to officers of the Polish army in a ceremony on the North Inch, after an earlier presentation of a commemorative tablet to 'the City and County of Perth' by General Marian Kukiel, Officer Commanding the Polish Forces in Scotland. The inscription on the plaque reads 'Presented by the General Officer Commanding, Officers and Men of the 1st Polish Army Corps, in grateful appreciation of the friendship extended to them in the city and county of Perth, where the Polish troops, after undergoing trials and hardships, were able to rally and continue with their Allies the fight for freedom and honour'.

The Lynedoch or 90th Regiment Memorial immediately after completion, 1895. It was unveiled in 1896 as a memorial to Thomas Graham, Lord Lynedoch, incorporating a drinking fountain and details of regimental history. Local objections led to the siting of the monument close to the river at the south-east corner of the Inch, rather than opposite Rose Terrace as had originally been intended. Note that the Inch is fulfilling its historic role as a place for drying washing (background, to the right of the memorial). Note also the bandstand, erected in 1891 at the expense of the Pullar family, but demolished in 1958.

Unveiling of the 90th Regiment Memorial by Lord Wolseley, 8 December 1896. Wolseley is fourth from the right. Garnet Wolseley fought in the Crimea, and commanded British forces during the Ashanti War (1873–4) and the latter stages of the Zulu War (1879–80). His Egyptian campaign of 1882 culminated in victory at Tel-el-Kebir, but he was unable to reach Khartoum in time to save General Gordon in 1885. At the time of this photograph Wolseley was Commander-in-Chief of the British army.

Homecoming of Black Watch Volunteers from the Boer War, Perth General station, 17 May 1901. This area is now the station car park, with the Station Hotel on the right. The featured troops were the 1st Volunteer Service Company, who were assembled in Perth in January 1900, and left for South Africa the following month. They arrived in Capetown on 11 March, and a month later were reinforcing the regular 2nd Battalion of the regiment, which had sustained heavy losses at the battle of Magersfontein in December 1899. The Volunteers fought alongside the 2nd Battalion for a year, and arrived back in Perth for demobilisation in May 1901.

'Perthshire Patriotic Barrow', Perth station, *c.* 1917. Perthshire Women's Patriotic Committee raised funds to provide free refreshments for servicemen in transit. The Hon. Treasurer of the Committee was James Shankland, of the British Linen Bank in Caledonian Road.

Unveiling a memorial to General Accident staff who had fallen in the First World War at the entrance to General Buildings, 1922. The memorial was taken to the new headquarters in 1983. A total of thirty-eight 'GA' staff died during the conflict. The *Perthshire Advertiser* opened a 'penny fund' to go towards the restoration of St John's Kirk as a memorial to Perthshire servicemen who had lost their lives in the war. The 'GA' was the first subscriber, donating 25,336 pennies. Note Eastman's basket-making premises at 8 High Street on the extreme right of the picture.

The Shrine, St John's Kirk, 1929. The Shrine is dedicated to the 3,670 men of Perth and Perthshire who died during the First World War. In the aftermath of the First World War a major programme of restoration work in the kirk was undertaken by Sir Robert Lorimer, part of which involved the removal of internal dividing walls. These had been erected in the eighteenth century to make what were effectively three separate churches, each with a minister; they were called the East, West and Middle parishes. Lorimer's work served to re-unify the interior of the kirk.

Pipes & Drums of the Black Watch, beating the retreat at the Queen's Barracks, 1937. Note St Ninian's Cathedral (built 1849–50) in the background, right. Army reforms of 1881 led to the formation of the 42nd Regimental District Headquarters at Queen's Barracks, and in 1904 the Regimental Depot was established there. When the barracks closed in 1962 all the Highland regiments began to train together at various locations. The barracks were demolished during the 1970s, and the site was subsequently taken up by part of the inner ring road, the police station, and Dewar Court – a development of British Legion housing.

HM Queen Elizabeth, Queen Mother – Colonel-in-Chief of the Black Watch since 1937 – unveils a stained glass memorial window in St John's Kirk, 24 August 1955. The window commemorates the sacrifice of those soldiers of 6th Battalion Black Watch who lost their lives during the Second World War. Accompanying the Queen Mother is the Revd W.A. Smellie BD (left) and the Lord Provost, James Alexander Smart.

Balhousie Castle, formerly a residence of the Earls of Kinnoull, and Museum and regimental HQ of the Black Watch since 1962. The original castle was built in the early fifteenth century for the Eviot family, and the present building dates largely from a restoration of 1864. The Regimental Museum receives around 10,000 visitors per year.

ATS Open Days, Balhousie Castle, 1943. Members of the Auxiliary Training Service were stationed in the castle during the Second World War. Before the conflict Balhousie had for some years been a convent, occupied by Episcopalian nuns attached to St Ninian's Cathedral. The impressive archway featured in the photograph is no longer in place, having been destroyed by the army during the war.

The Robert Douglas Memorial School in Scone served as the headquarters for Polish troops in the area, a fact commemorated by a Polish eagle on the front of the building.

Laying up the old Colours of the 1st Battalion, Black Watch, 21 June 1978. Members of 1st Battalion are marching down the High Street from their assembly point on the site of the old barracks towards Balhousie Castle. The parade is being led by company commander Major Edward de Broe-Ferguson. The Colours had been presented by Field Marshall Earl Wavell, Colonel of the regiment, at Duisburg in August 1947, and were carried until 1975.

The war memorial on North Inch, 1995. The memorial by Alan Beattie Heriot depicts a small Dutch girl handing a bouquet of flowers to a soldier of the 51st Highland Division, after the liberation of the town of Eerde. It was constructed to commemorate the fiftieth anniversary of the ending of the Second World War in Europe, and an identical memorial stands in Eerde.

Lipton's shop, High Street, Perth, *c.* 1890.

*Looking for a picture to hang on the wall, an image for research or just to remember?
Contact*

> Perth Museum and Art Gallery
> George Street
> Perth
> Tayside
> PH2 6DA

We also have fine collections and striking exhibitions of history, natural science and art.

ACKNOWLEDGEMENTS

We would like to offer our sincere thanks to the following individuals for their interest, enthusiasm, support and shared knowledge during the production of this book:

Anne Brodie, Michael Bullough, Owen Boyle of the County Hotel, Fraser Campbell, Rhona Campbell, Douglas Davidson, Norman Dickson, Arthur Duvay, Simon Fletcher, Louis Flood, Benny Gillies, Vicky Gudmundsson, Stewart Harris of the Tayside Police Museum, Susan Hendry of Perth Civic Trust, Robin Keay of the *Perthshire Advertiser*, Stan Kirkpatrick, David Leggatt of United Auctions, Lieutenant-Colonel Stephen Lindsay, Hazel McFadzean of Perthshire Agricultural Society, Aoife Martin of United Distillers & Vintners, Eileen Primrose, Major D.B. Pover, Jacqui Sargeant of John Dewar & Sons Ltd, Donald Smith, Thomas Smyth, Martin Young of A. & G. Cairncross Ltd, the staff of Perth Museum and Art Gallery, and of the Local Studies section of the A.K. Bell Library.

Particular thanks are due to Susan Payne, Principal Officer of Human History, Perth Museum & Art Gallery, to Tom Berthon, for generously sharing his photographs of more recent 'old Perth', and to Stan Keay, for applying his eagle eye and wealth of local knowledge to the text.

Photographs are reproduced by kind permission of the following:

Tom Berthon: pp. 7, 10, 11 (upper), 13 (upper), 19 (lower), 25 (upper), 19 (lower), 25 (upper), 30, 31 (upper), 34 (lower), 40 (upper), 47 (upper), 48, 51, 62 (lower), 65 (lower), 66 (lower), 70 (upper), 71 (upper), 75, 79 (upper), 82 (upper), 90, 96 (lower), 97 (upper), 106 (lower), 110 (upper), 117.

Owen Boyle: p. 73 (lower).

A. & G. Cairncross Ltd: p. 70 (lower).

CGNU plc: pp. 59, 68 (upper), 96 (upper), 97 (upper), 106 (lower), 110 (upper), 117.

John Dewar & Sons Ltd: pp. 55 (lower), 56, 57 (upper), 82 (lower), 102 (lower), 120 (lower), 122 (lower).

Douglas Davidson: p. 72 (upper).

Norman Dickson: p. 68 (lower).

Benny Gillies: pp. 14 (upper), 41 (upper).

Perth Museum and Art Gallery: pp: 14, 15 (upper), 18, 20, 24, 28 (lower), 33, 34 (upper), 35, 36 (lower), 40 (lower), 42, 43, 44 (upper), 49, 58 (lower), 60 (upper), 61 (upper), 64, 66 (upper), 71 (lower), 79 (lower), 80, 81, 84 (lower), 85 (lower), 86 (upper), 88, 92, 93, 94 (upper), 95, 106 (upper), 107 (upper), 108 (lower), 109, 114 (lower), 115, 120 (upper).

Tayside Police Museum: pp. 86 (lower), 87.

Trustees of the Black Watch Museum: pp. 89 (lower), 103, 121, 123, 124 (lower).

United Distillers & Vintners: pp. 54, 55 (upper), 63, 101 (lower), 108 (upper).

Many of the Victorian photographs included in this book were taken by Magnus Jackson, to whom Perth owes a great debt of gratitude for capturing images which have become so valuable to historians and lovers of the Fair City.